Take A Walk, Beetle Bailey ®

by Mort Walker

JOVE BOOKS, NEW YORK

TAKE A WALK, BEETLE BAILEY

A Jove Book / published by arrangement with
King Features Syndicate, Inc.

PRINTING HISTORY
Tempo edition / July 1976
Charter edition / July 1986
Jove edition / August 1987

For information address: The Berkley Publishing Group, 200 Madison Avenue, New York, New York 10016.

ISBN: 0-515-09623-7

Jove Books are published by The Berkley Publishing Group, 200 Madison Avenue, New York, New York 10016.
The name "JOVE" and the "J" logo are trademarks belonging to Jove Publications, Inc.
PRINTED IN THE UNITED STATES OF AMERICA

10 9 8 7 6 5 4 3 2

Take A Walk, Beetle Bailey

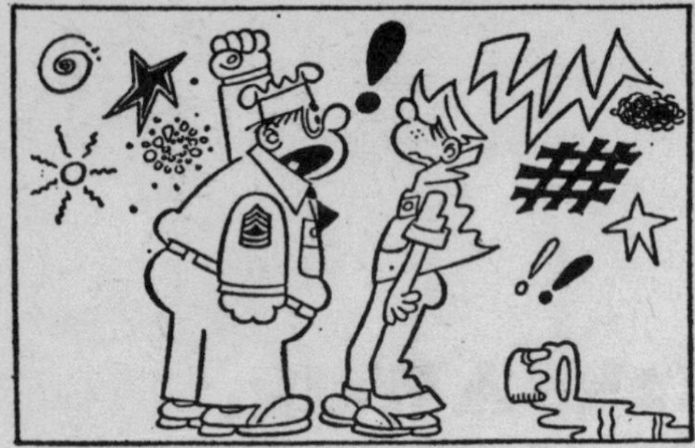

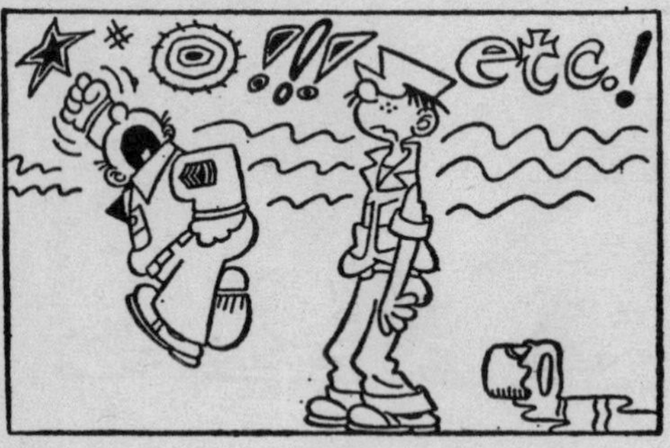
etc.!

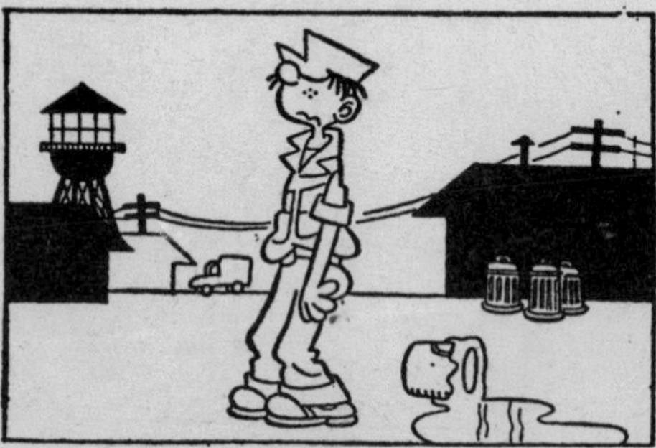

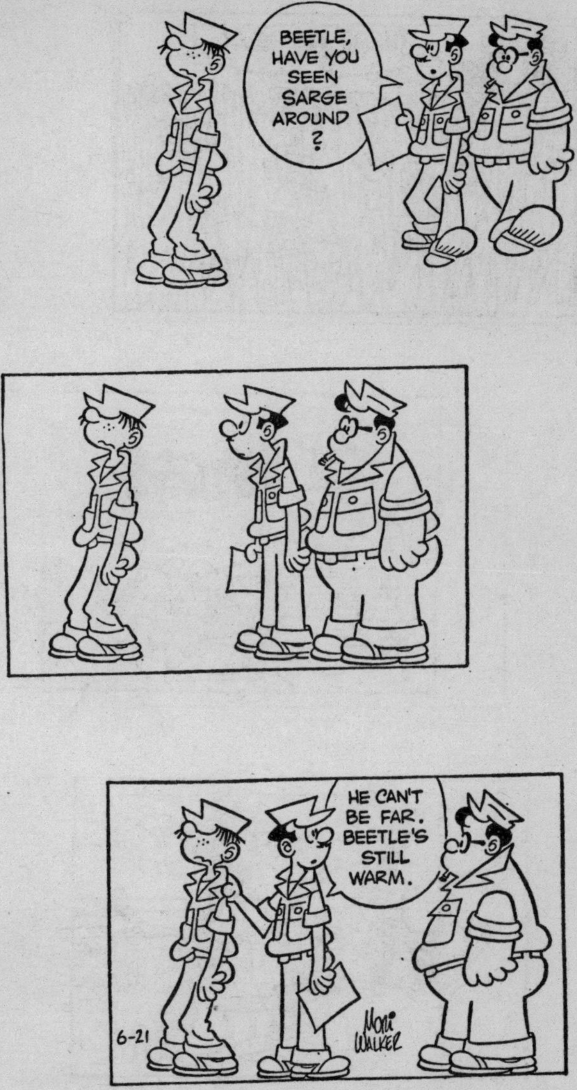
BEETLE, HAVE YOU SEEN SARGE AROUND?
HE CAN'T BE FAR. BEETLE'S STILL WARM.
6-21
MORT WALKER

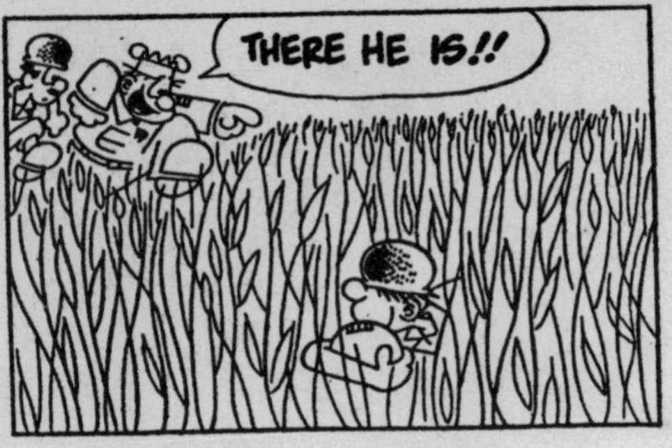
THERE HE IS!!

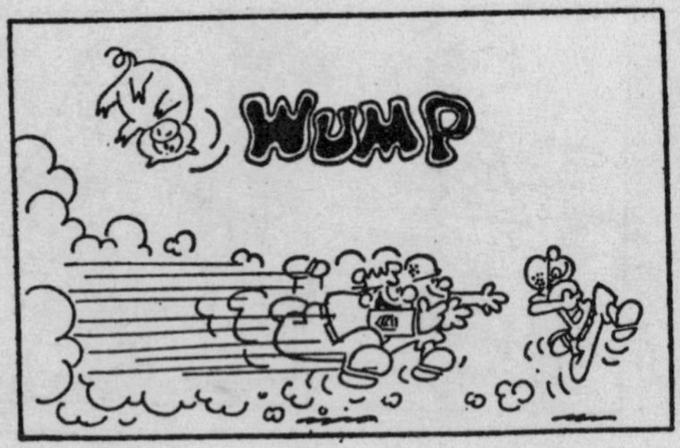
WUMP

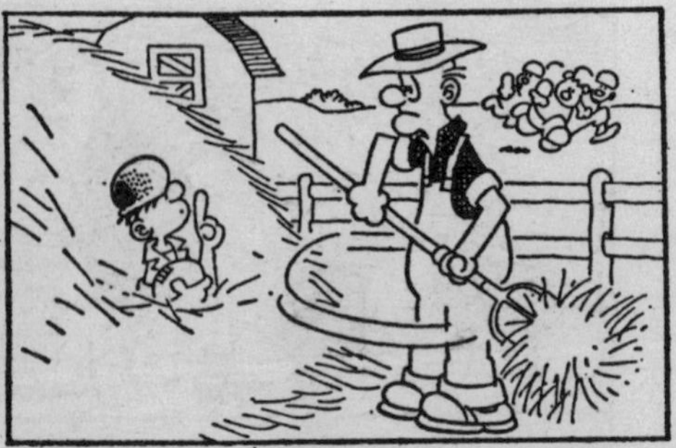

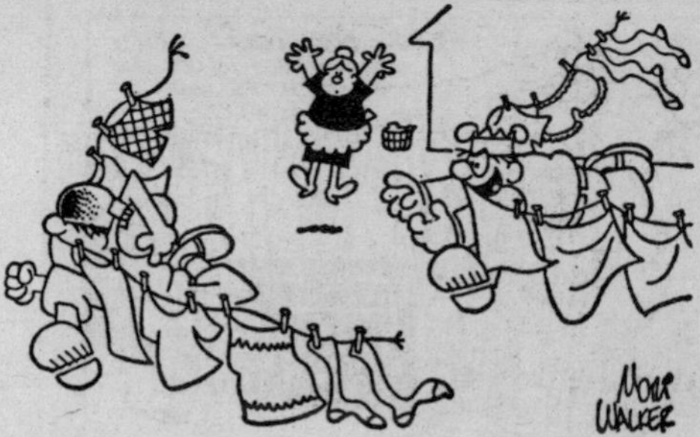
MORT WALKER

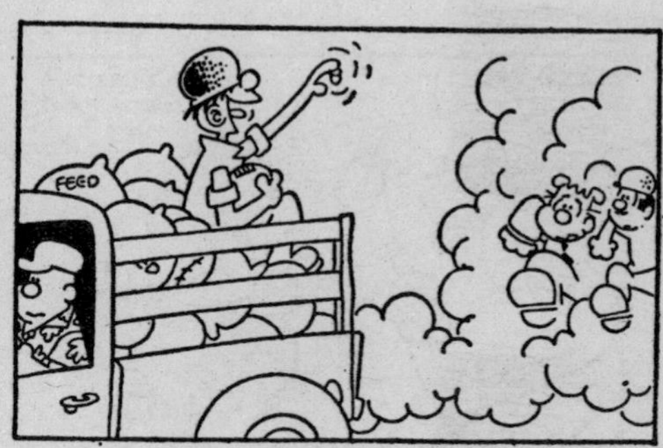
FEED

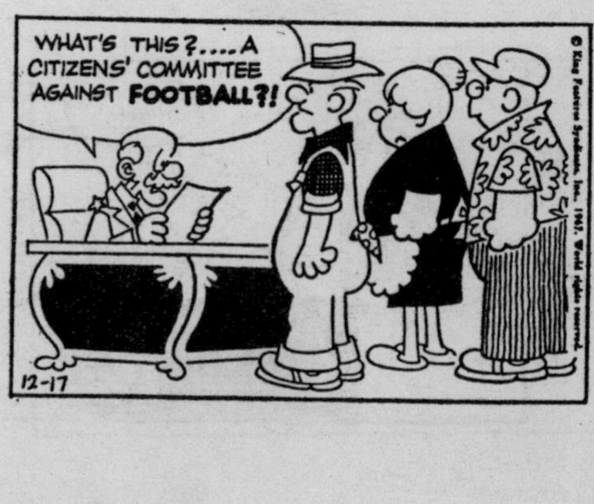
WHAT'S THIS?....A CITIZENS' COMMITTEE AGAINST FOOTBALL?!
12-17
© King Features Syndicate, Inc., 1967. World rights reserved.

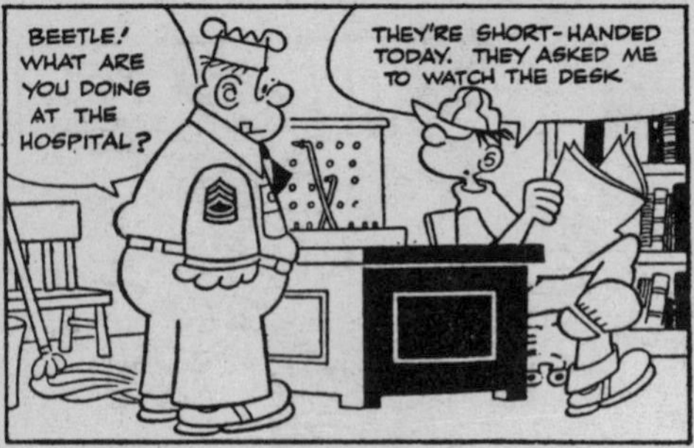
BEETLE! WHAT ARE YOU DOING AT THE HOSPITAL?
THEY'RE SHORT-HANDED TODAY. THEY ASKED ME TO WATCH THE DESK

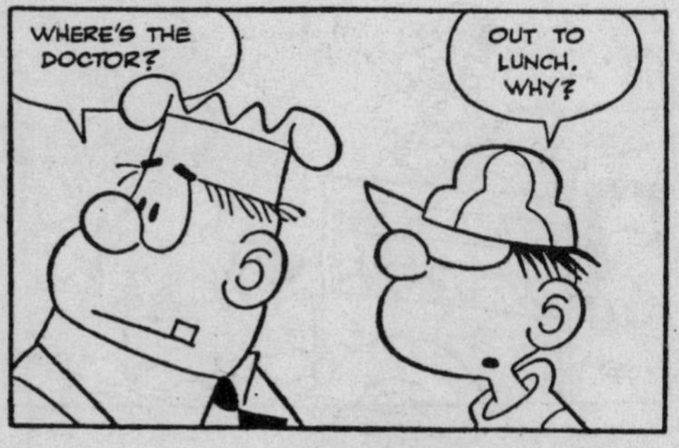
WHERE'S THE DOCTOR?
OUT TO LUNCH. WHY?

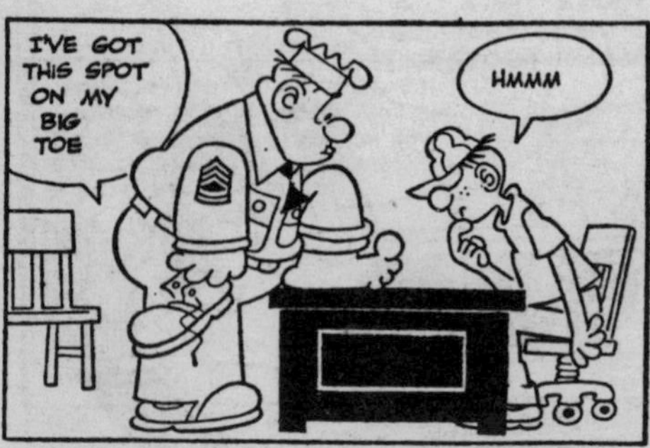
I'VE GOT THIS SPOT ON MY BIG TOE
HMMM

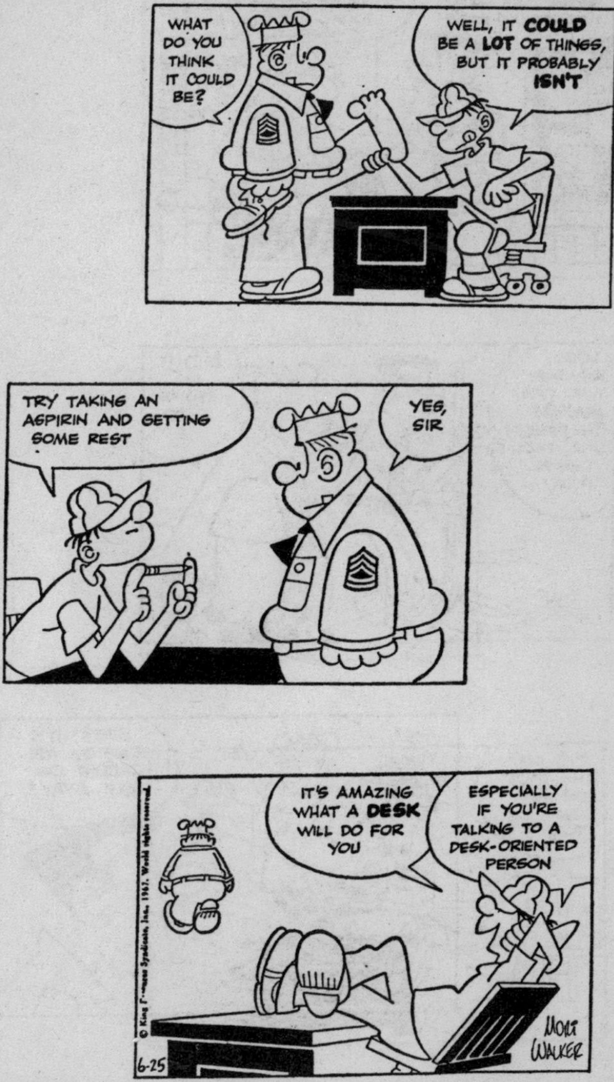
WHAT DO YOU THINK IT COULD BE?
WELL, IT **COULD** BE A **LOT** OF THINGS, BUT IT PROBABLY **ISN'T**
TRY TAKING AN ASPIRIN AND GETTING SOME REST
YES, SIR
IT'S AMAZING WHAT A **DESK** WILL DO FOR YOU
ESPECIALLY IF YOU'RE TALKING TO A DESK-ORIENTED PERSON
6-25
MORT WALKER

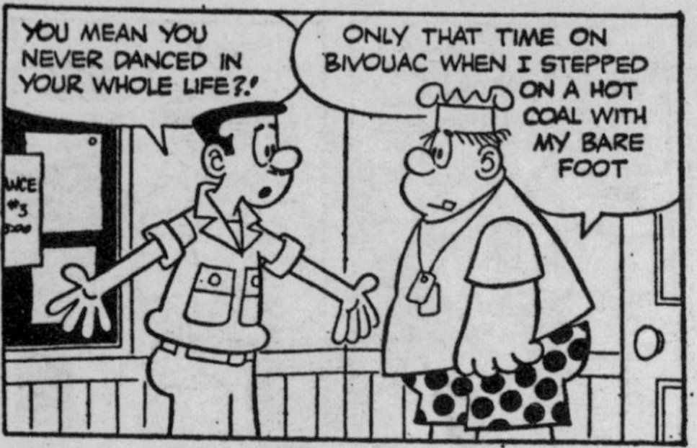
YOU MEAN YOU NEVER DANCED IN YOUR WHOLE LIFE?!
ONLY THAT TIME ON BIVOUAC WHEN I STEPPED ON A HOT COAL WITH MY BARE FOOT

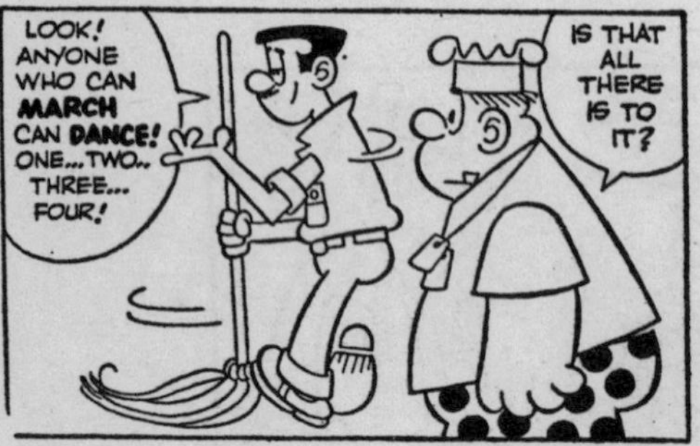
LOOK! ANYONE WHO CAN **MARCH** CAN **DANCE!** ONE...TWO.. THREE... FOUR!
IS THAT ALL THERE IS TO IT?

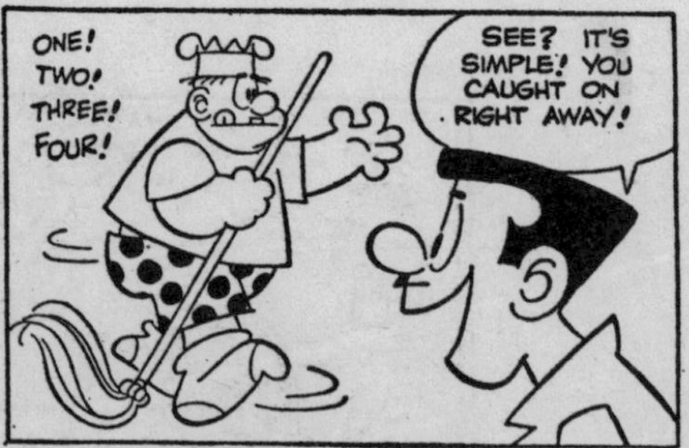
ONE! TWO! THREE! FOUR!
SEE? IT'S SIMPLE! YOU CAUGHT ON RIGHT AWAY!

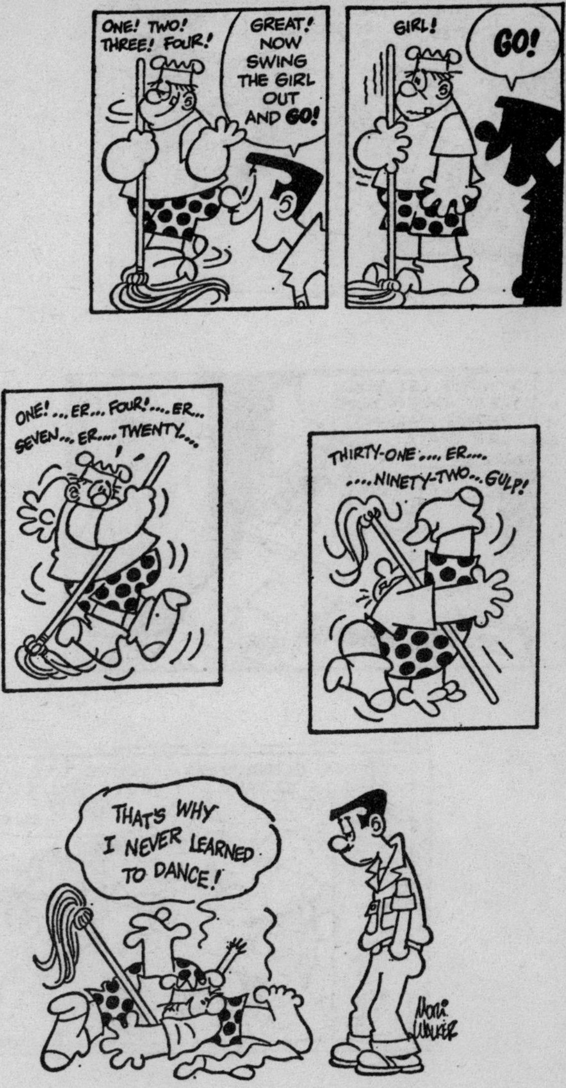
ONE! TWO! THREE! FOUR!
GREAT! NOW SWING THE GIRL OUT AND GO!
GIRL!
GO!
ONE! ... ER ... FOUR! .... ER ... SEVEN ... ER .... TWENTY ....
THIRTY-ONE .... ER .... NINETY-TWO ... GULP!
THAT'S WHY I NEVER LEARNED TO DANCE!
MORT WALKER

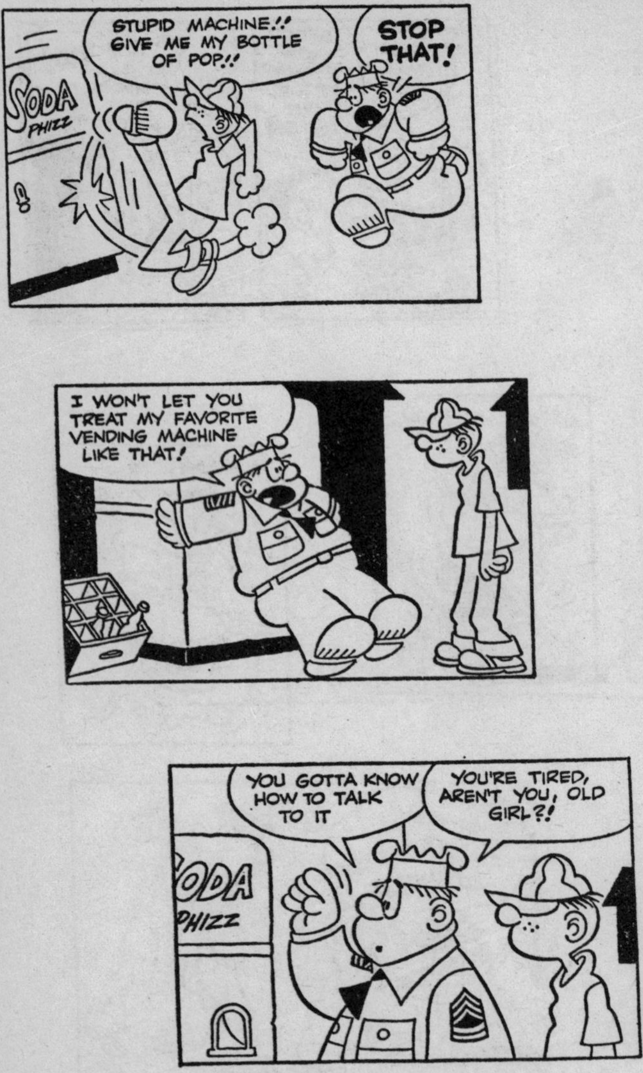
SODA PHIZZ
STUPID MACHINE!! GIVE ME MY BOTTLE OF POP!!
STOP THAT!
I WON'T LET YOU TREAT MY FAVORITE VENDING MACHINE LIKE THAT!
SODA PHIZZ
YOU GOTTA KNOW HOW TO TALK TO IT
YOU'RE TIRED, AREN'T YOU, OLD GIRL?!

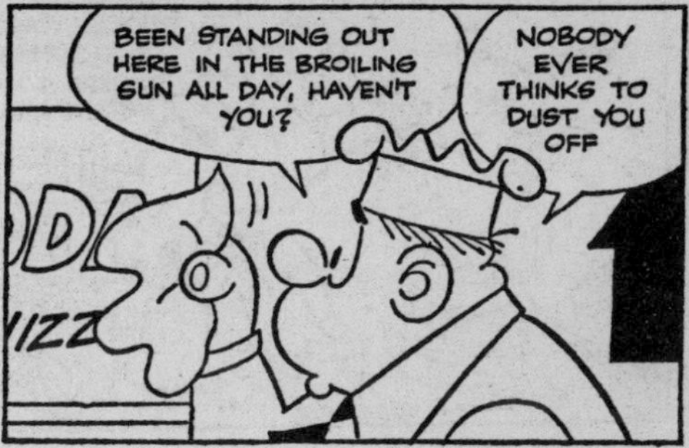
BEEN STANDING OUT HERE IN THE BROILING SUN ALL DAY, HAVEN'T YOU?
NOBODY EVER THINKS TO DUST YOU OFF

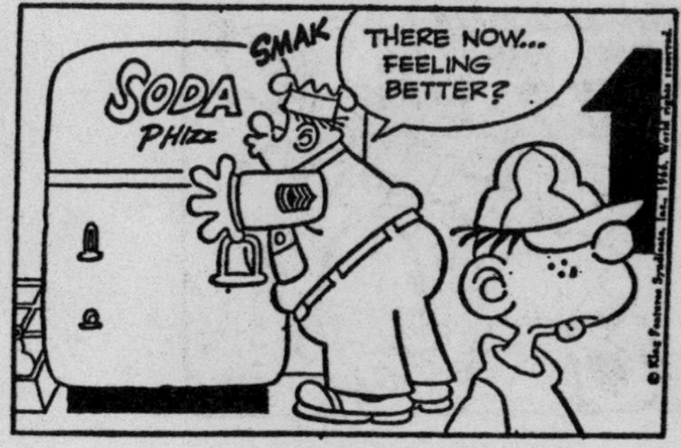
SMAK
THERE NOW... FEELING BETTER?
SODA
PHIZZ

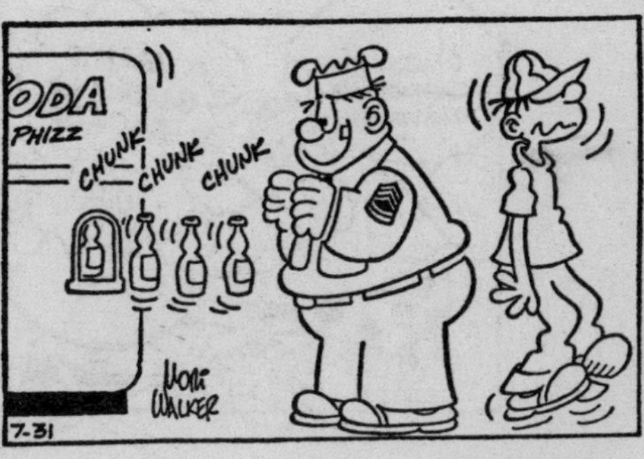
ODA
PHIZZ
CHUNK
CHUNK
CHUNK
MORT WALKER
7-31

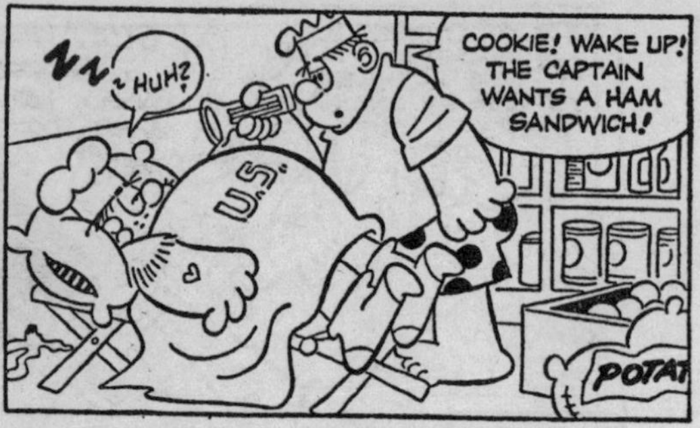
ZZ
HUH?
COOKIE! WAKE UP! THE CAPTAIN WANTS A HAM SANDWICH!
U.S.
POTAT

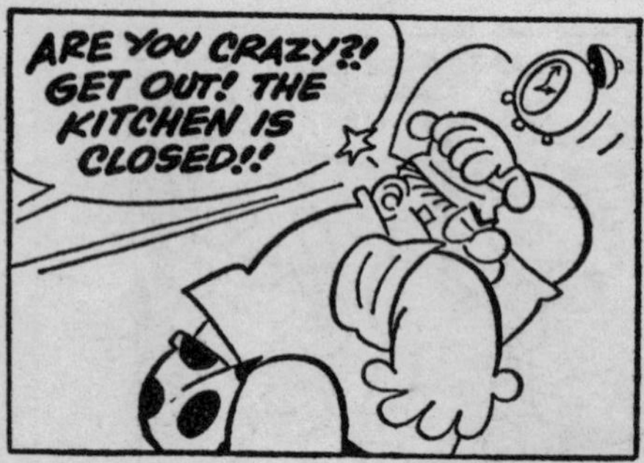
ARE YOU CRAZY?! GET OUT! THE KITCHEN IS CLOSED!!

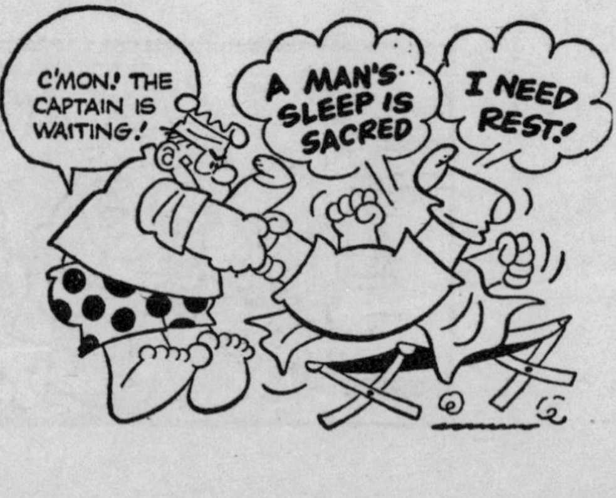
C'MON! THE CAPTAIN IS WAITING!
A MAN'S SLEEP IS SACRED
I NEED REST!

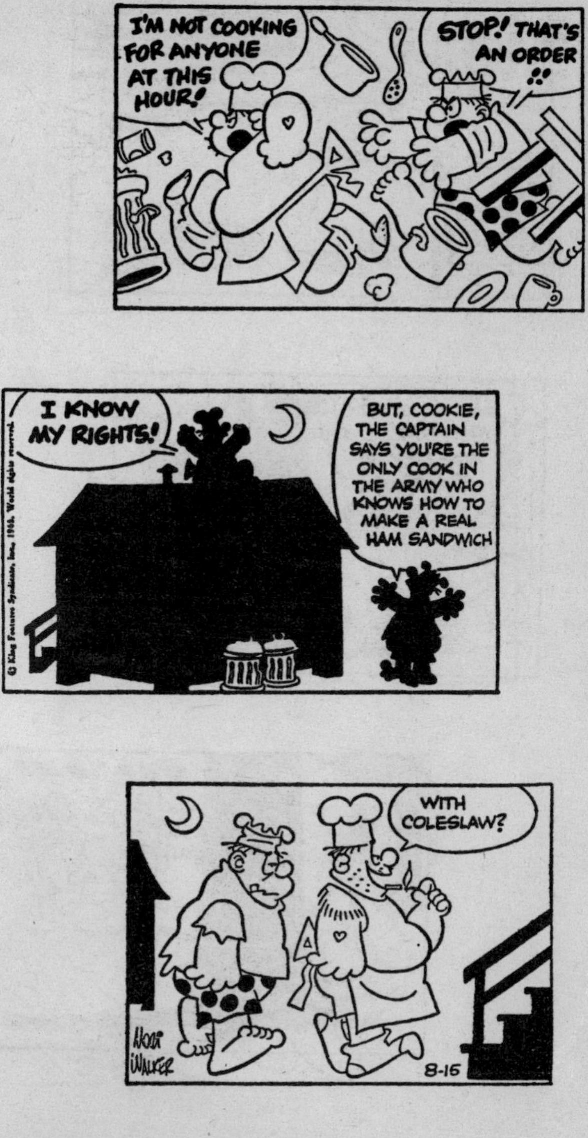
I'M NOT COOKING FOR ANYONE AT THIS HOUR!
STOP! THAT'S AN ORDER !!
I KNOW MY RIGHTS!
BUT, COOKIE, THE CAPTAIN SAYS YOU'RE THE ONLY COOK IN THE ARMY WHO KNOWS HOW TO MAKE A REAL HAM SANDWICH
WITH COLESLAW?
© King Features Syndicate, Inc. World rights reserved.
MORT WALKER
8-15

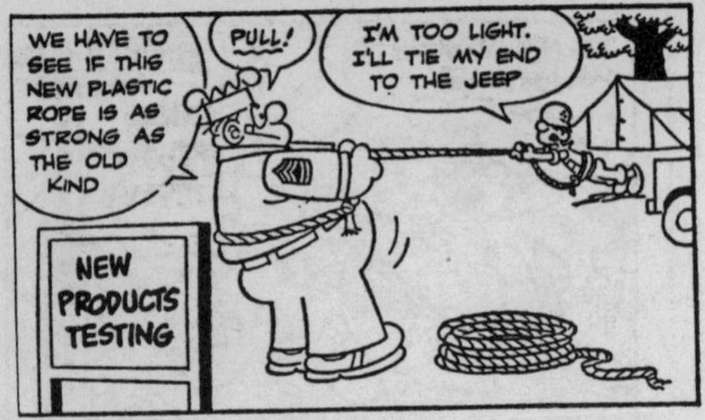
WE HAVE TO SEE IF THIS NEW PLASTIC ROPE IS AS STRONG AS THE OLD KIND
PULL!
I'M TOO LIGHT. I'LL TIE MY END TO THE JEEP
NEW PRODUCTS TESTING

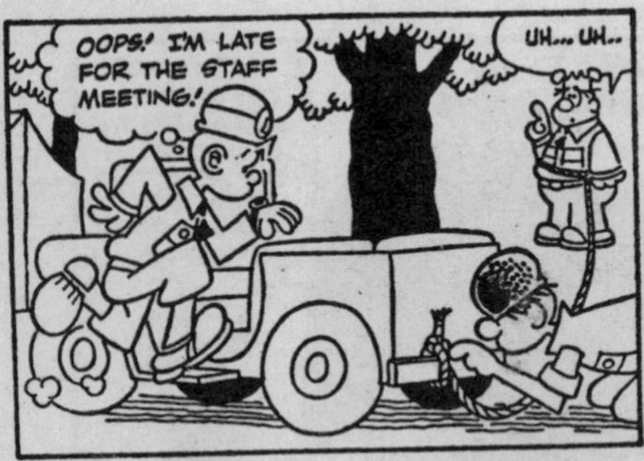
OOPS! I'M LATE FOR THE STAFF MEETING!
UH... UH..

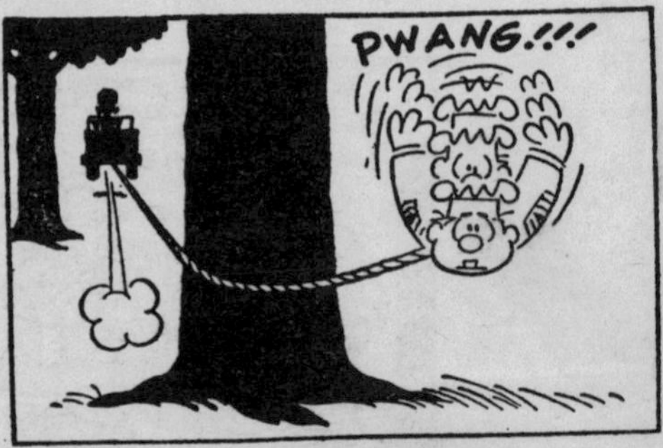
PWANG!!!!

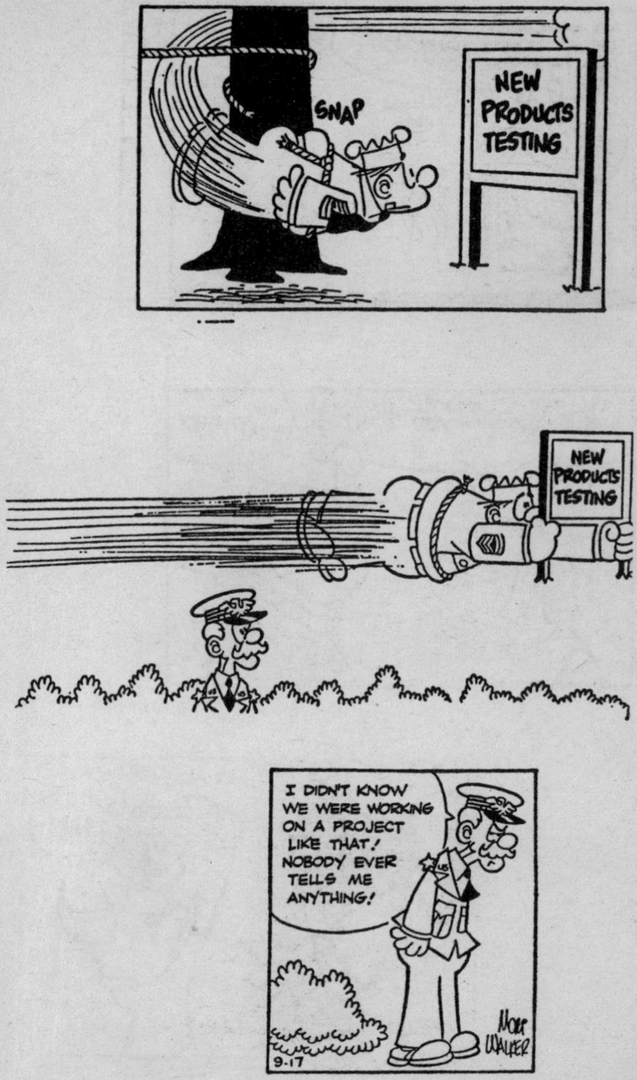
SNAP
NEW PRODUCTS TESTING
NEW PRODUCTS TESTING
I DIDN'T KNOW WE WERE WORKING ON A PROJECT LIKE THAT! NOBODY EVER TELLS ME ANYTHING!
MORT WALKER
9-17

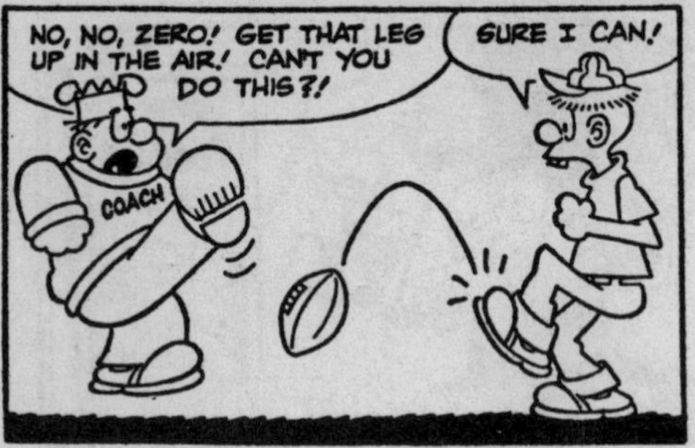
NO, NO, ZERO! GET THAT LEG UP IN THE AIR! CAN'T YOU DO THIS?!
SURE I CAN!
COACH

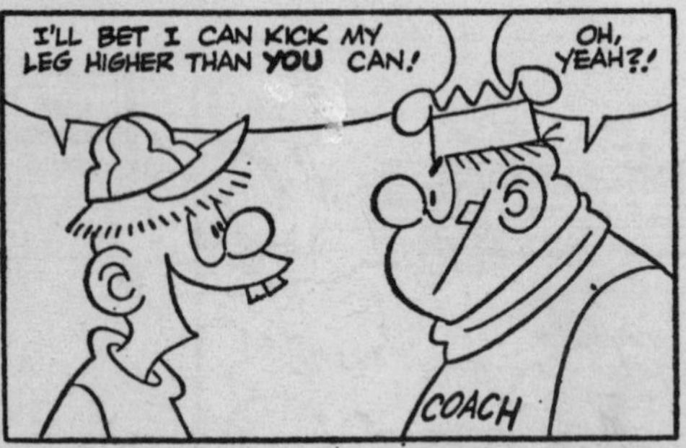
I'LL BET I CAN KICK MY LEG HIGHER THAN YOU CAN!
OH, YEAH?!
COACH

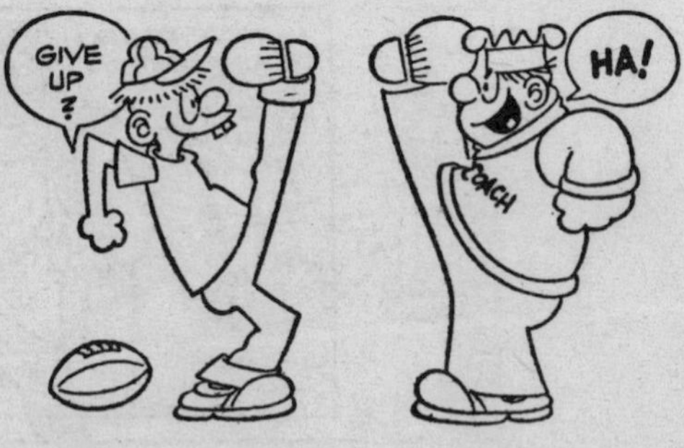
GIVE UP ?
HA!
COACH

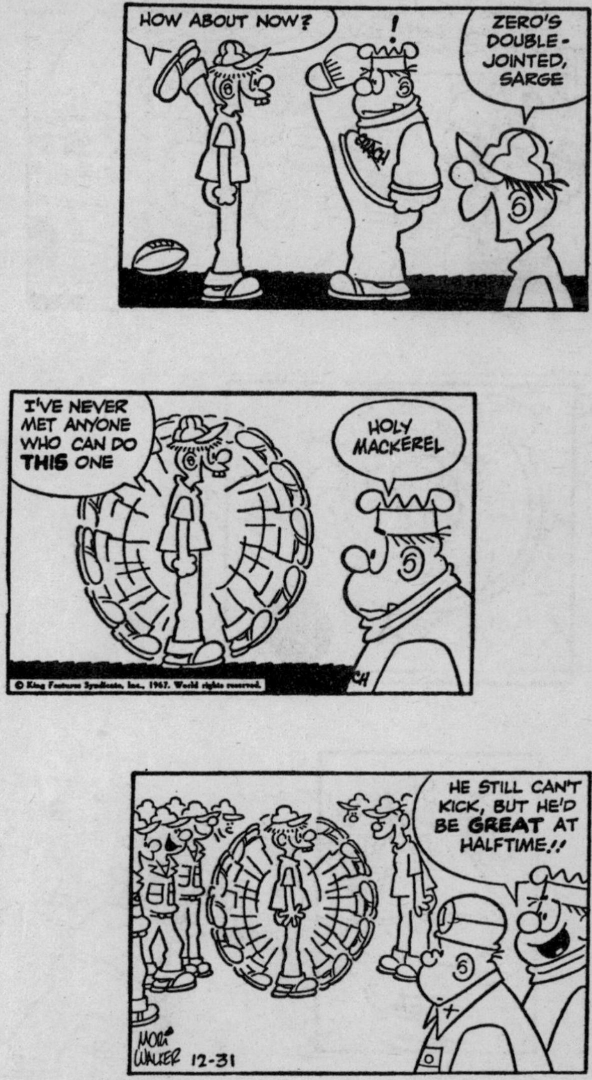
HOW ABOUT NOW?
!
ZERO'S DOUBLE-JOINTED, SARGE
COACH
I'VE NEVER MET ANYONE WHO CAN DO **THIS** ONE
HOLY MACKEREL
© King Features Syndicate, Inc., 1967. World rights reserved.
HE STILL CAN'T KICK, BUT HE'D BE **GREAT** AT HALFTIME!!
MORT WALKER 12-31

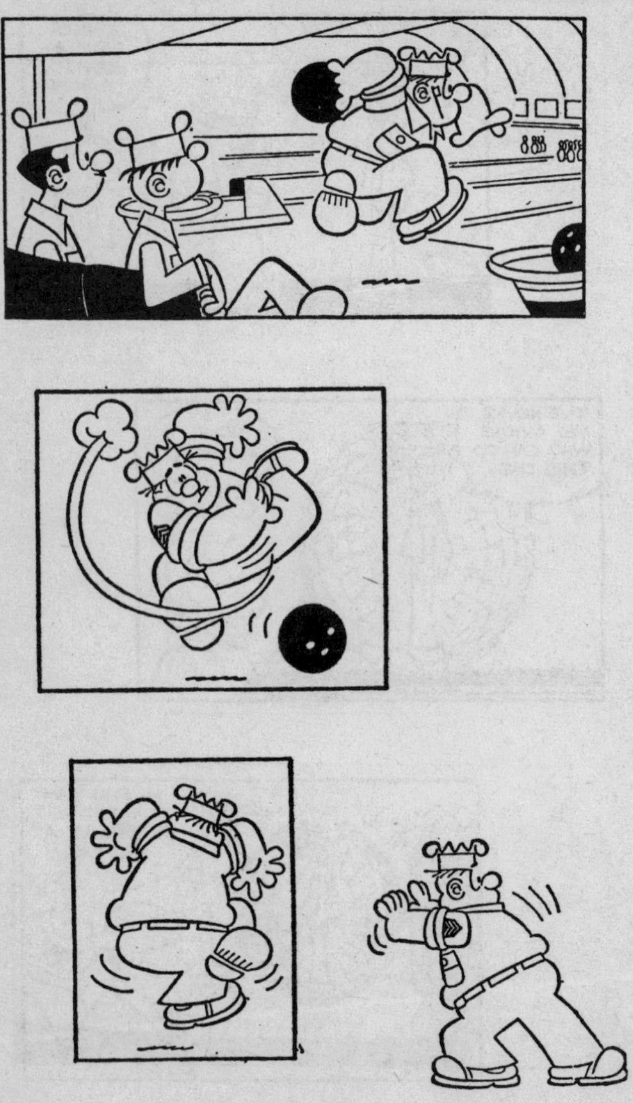

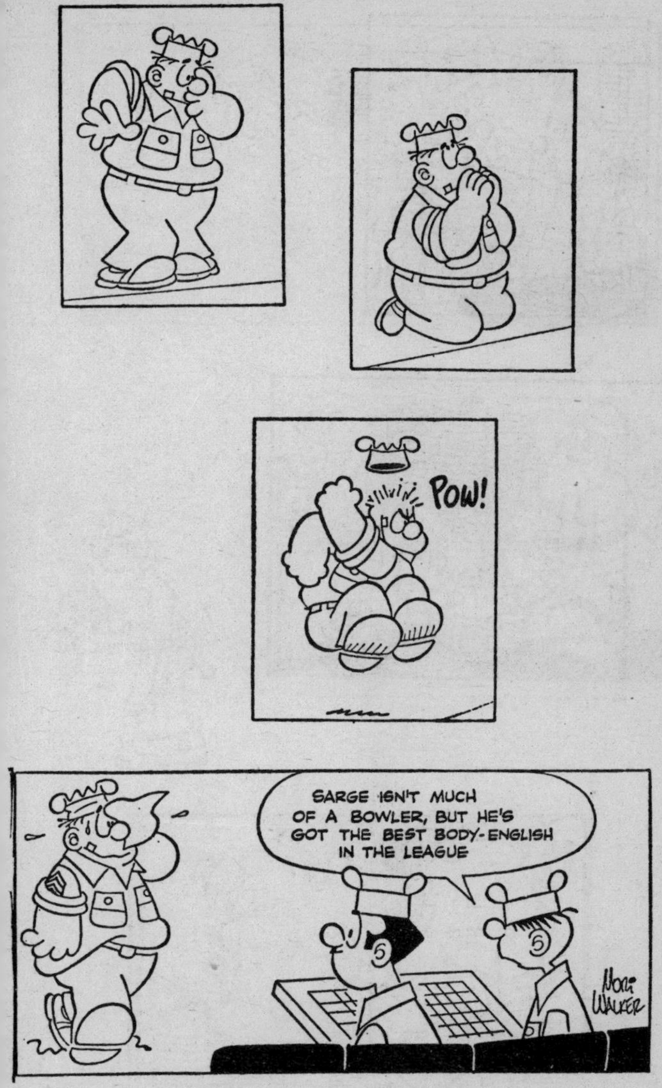
POW!
SARGE ISN'T MUCH OF A BOWLER, BUT HE'S GOT THE BEST BODY-ENGLISH IN THE LEAGUE
MORT WALKER

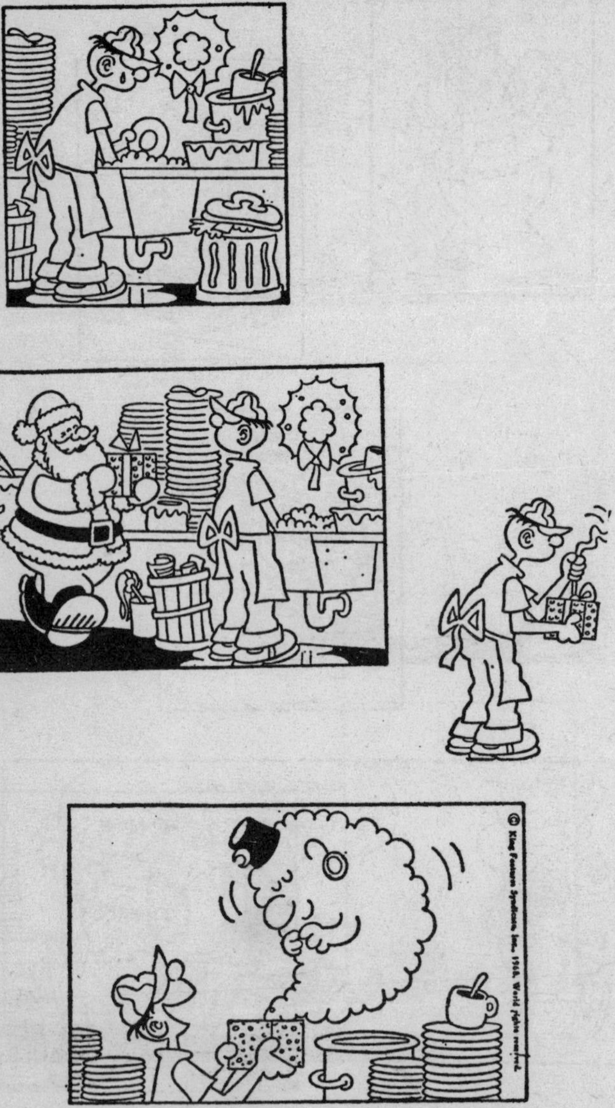
© King Features Syndicate, Inc., 1968. World rights reserved.

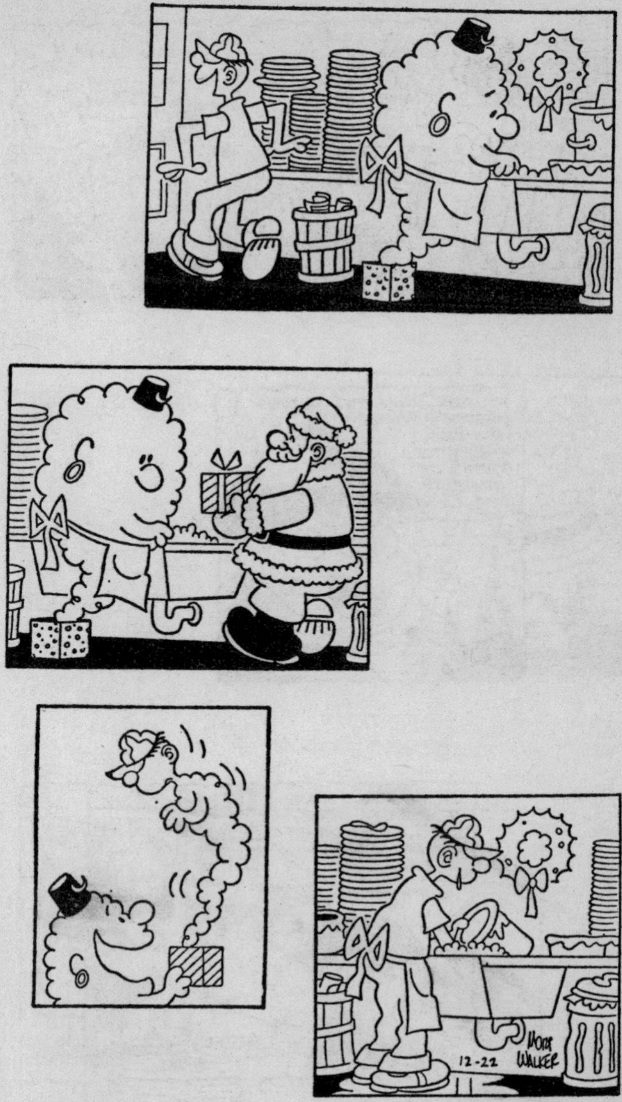
12-22
MORT WALKER

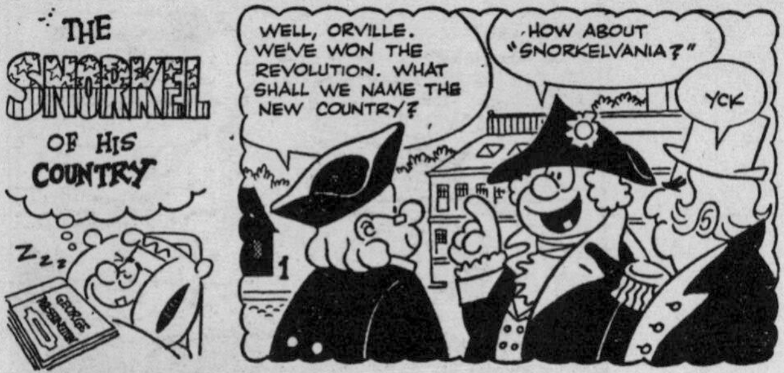
THE SNORKEL OF HIS COUNTRY
WELL, ORVILLE. WE'VE WON THE REVOLUTION. WHAT SHALL WE NAME THE NEW COUNTRY?
HOW ABOUT "SNORKELVANIA?"
YCK

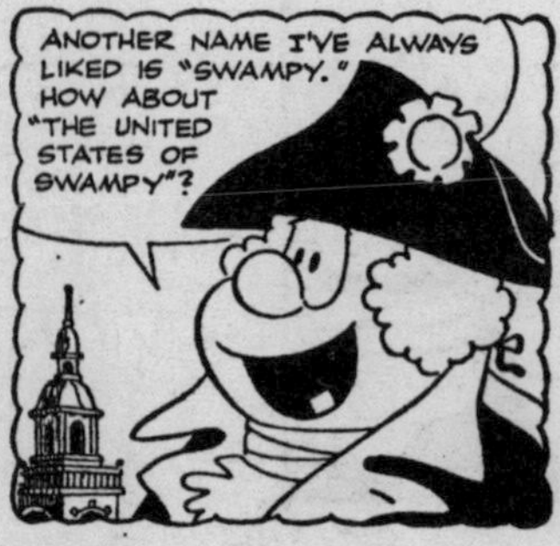
ANOTHER NAME I'VE ALWAYS LIKED IS "SWAMPY." HOW ABOUT "THE UNITED STATES OF SWAMPY"?

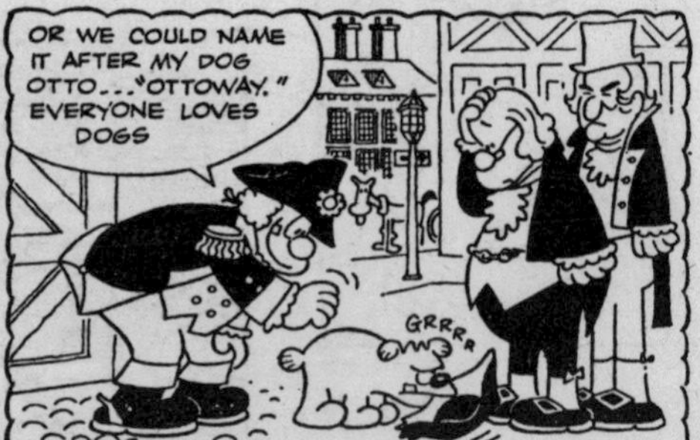
OR WE COULD NAME IT AFTER MY DOG OTTO..."OTTOWAY." EVERYONE LOVES DOGS
GRRRR

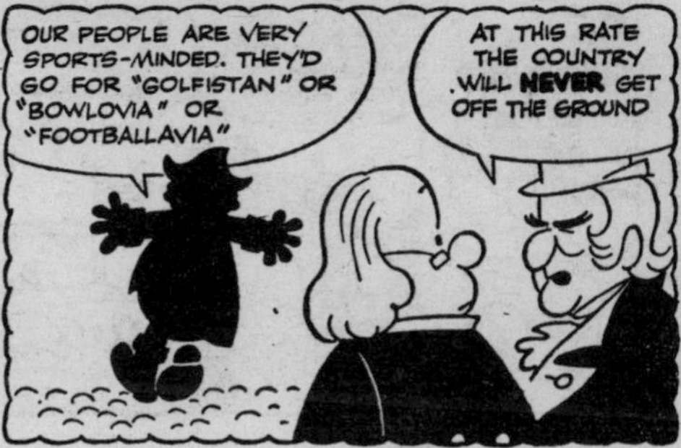
OUR PEOPLE ARE VERY SPORTS-MINDED. THEY'D GO FOR "GOLFISTAN" OR "BOWLOVIA" OR "FOOTBALLAVIA"
AT THIS RATE THE COUNTRY WILL **NEVER** GET OFF THE GROUND

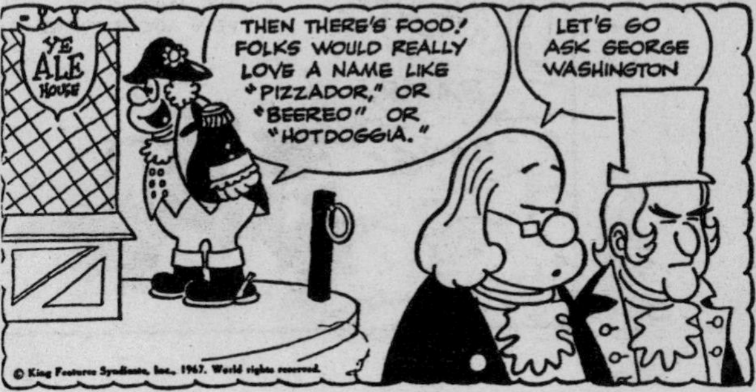
YE ALE HOUSE
THEN THERE'S FOOD! FOLKS WOULD REALLY LOVE A NAME LIKE "PIZZADOR," OR "BEEREO" OR "HOTDOGGIA."
LET'S GO ASK GEORGE WASHINGTON

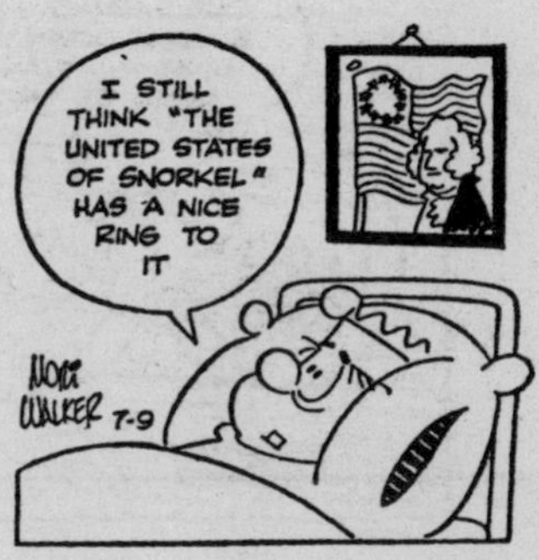
I STILL THINK "THE UNITED STATES OF SNORKEL" HAS A NICE RING TO IT
MORT WALKER 7-9

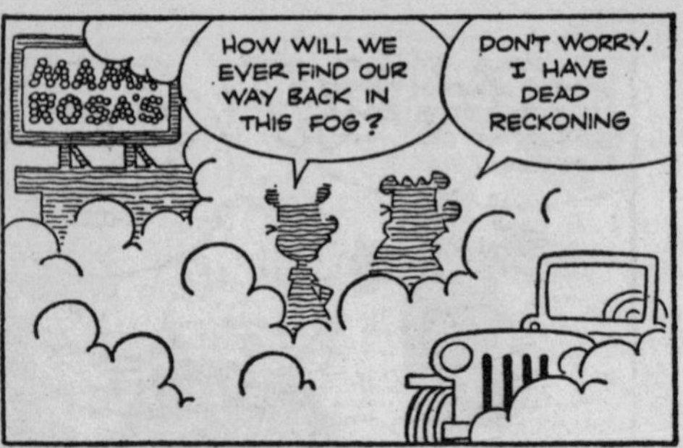
ROSA'S
HOW WILL WE EVER FIND OUR WAY BACK IN THIS FOG?
DON'T WORRY. I HAVE DEAD RECKONING

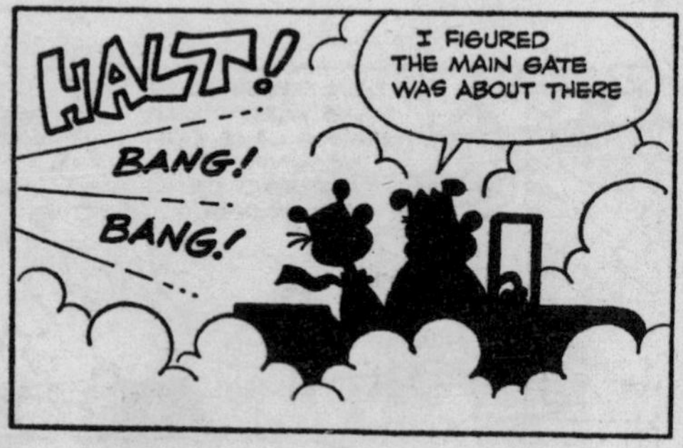
HALT!
I FIGURED THE MAIN GATE WAS ABOUT THERE
BANG!
BANG!

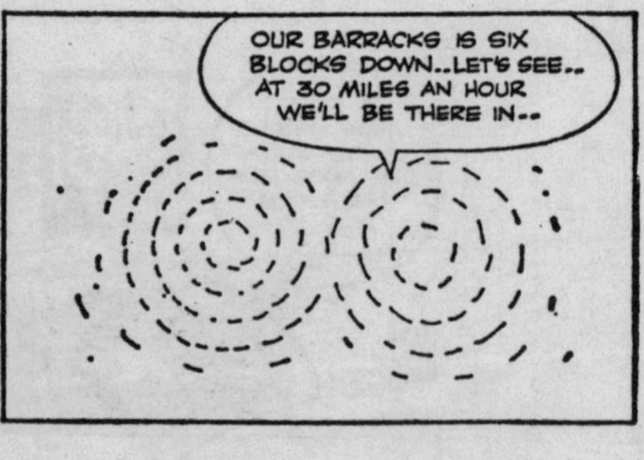
OUR BARRACKS IS SIX BLOCKS DOWN..LET'S SEE.. AT 30 MILES AN HOUR WE'LL BE THERE IN..

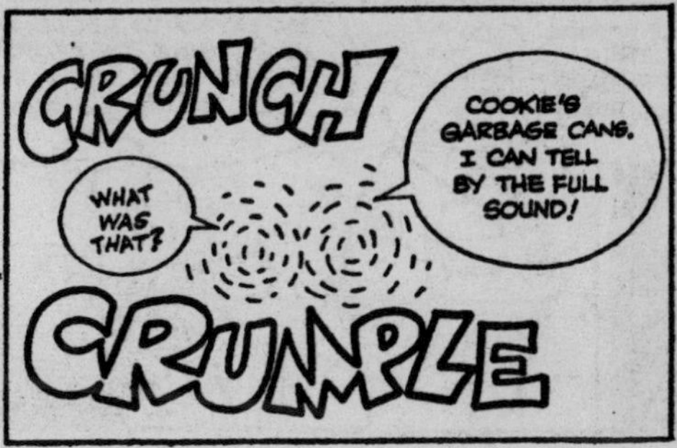
CRUNCH
WHAT WAS THAT?
COOKIE'S GARBAGE CANS. I CAN TELL BY THE FULL SOUND!
CRUMPLE

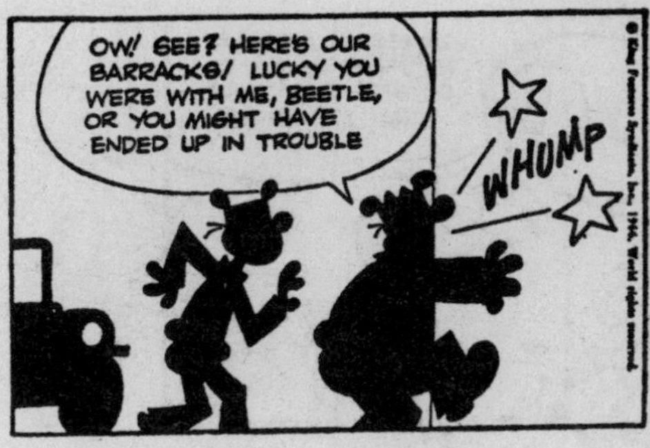
OW! SEE? HERE'S OUR BARRACKS! LUCKY YOU WERE WITH ME, BEETLE, OR YOU MIGHT HAVE ENDED UP IN TROUBLE
WHUMP

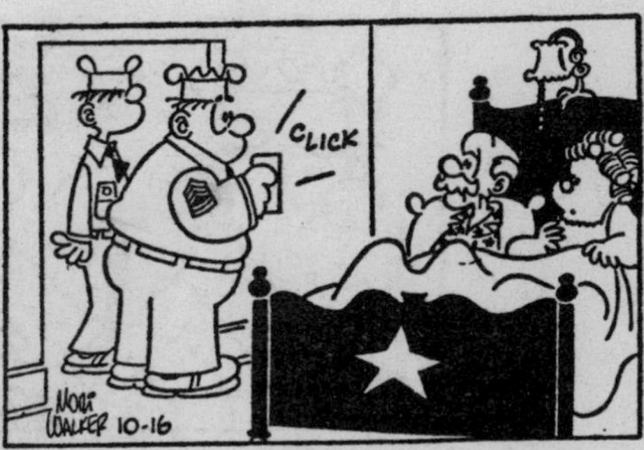
CLICK
MORT WALKER 10-16

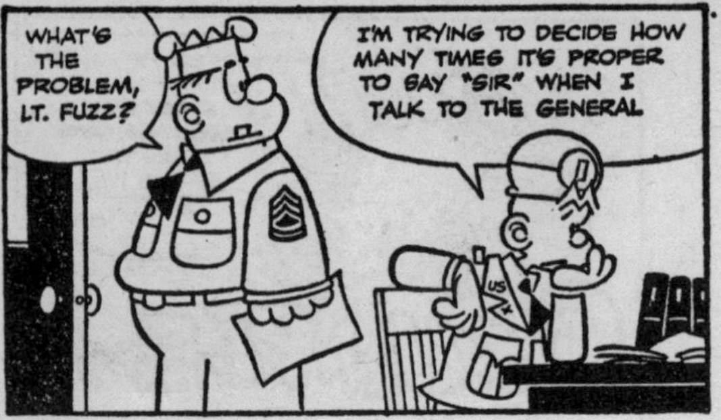
WHAT'S THE PROBLEM, LT. FUZZ?
I'M TRYING TO DECIDE HOW MANY TIMES IT'S PROPER TO SAY "SIR" WHEN I TALK TO THE GENERAL

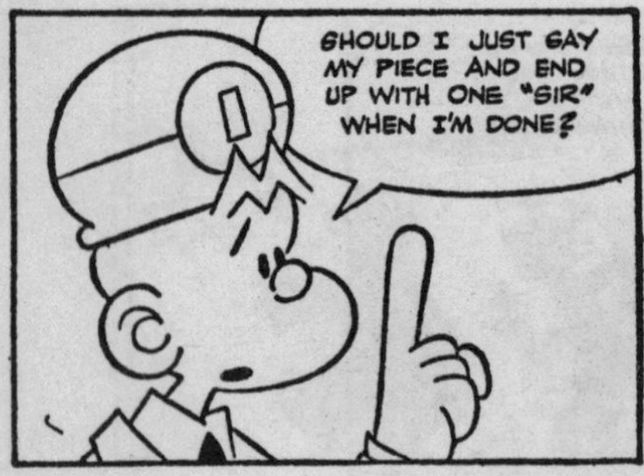
SHOULD I JUST SAY MY PIECE AND END UP WITH ONE "SIR" WHEN I'M DONE?

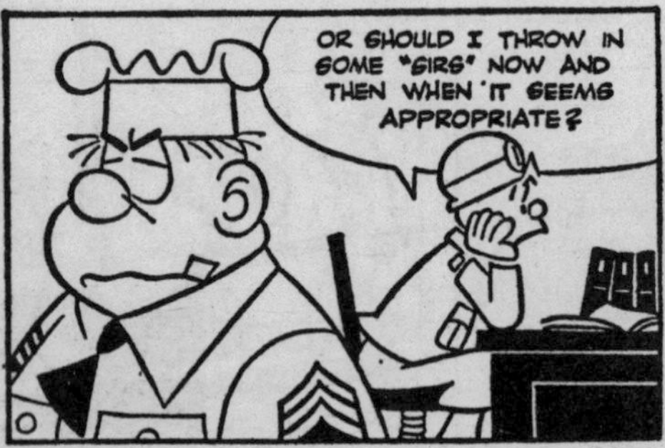
OR SHOULD I THROW IN SOME "SIRS" NOW AND THEN WHEN IT SEEMS APPROPRIATE?

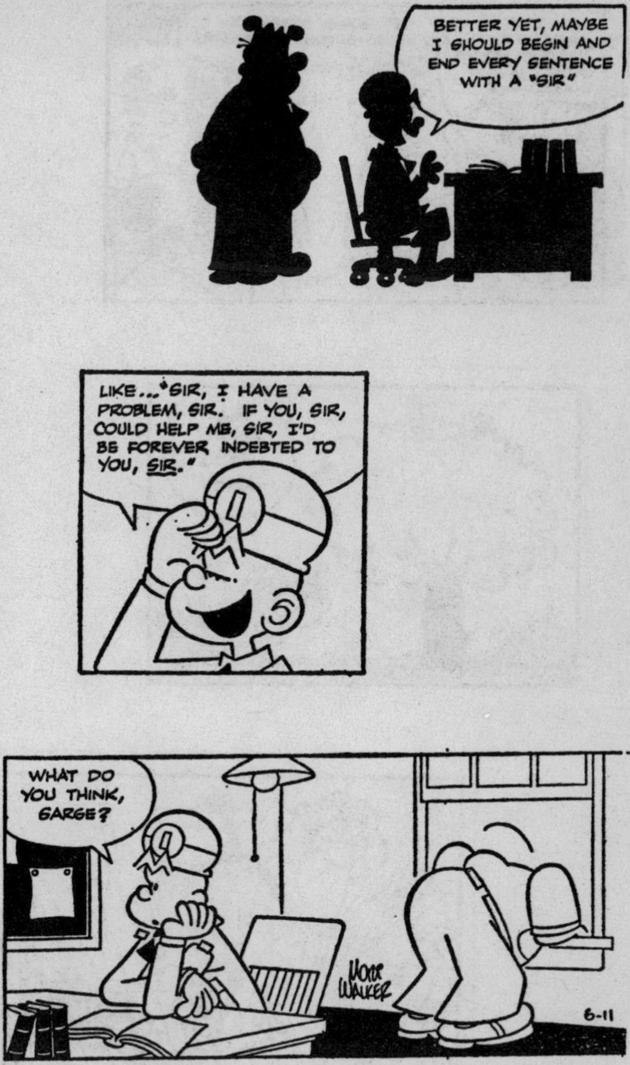
BETTER YET, MAYBE I SHOULD BEGIN AND END EVERY SENTENCE WITH A "SIR"
LIKE... "SIR, I HAVE A PROBLEM, SIR. IF YOU, SIR, COULD HELP ME, SIR, I'D BE FOREVER INDEBTED TO YOU, SIR."
WHAT DO YOU THINK, SARGE?
MORT WALKER
6-11

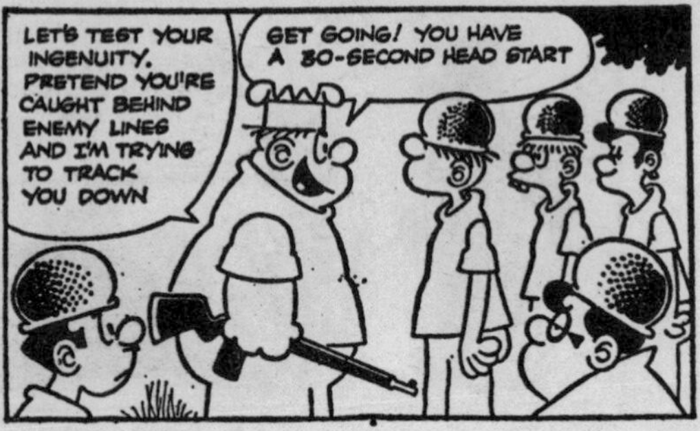
LET'S TEST YOUR INGENUITY. PRETEND YOU'RE CAUGHT BEHIND ENEMY LINES AND I'M TRYING TO TRACK YOU DOWN
GET GOING! YOU HAVE A 30-SECOND HEAD START

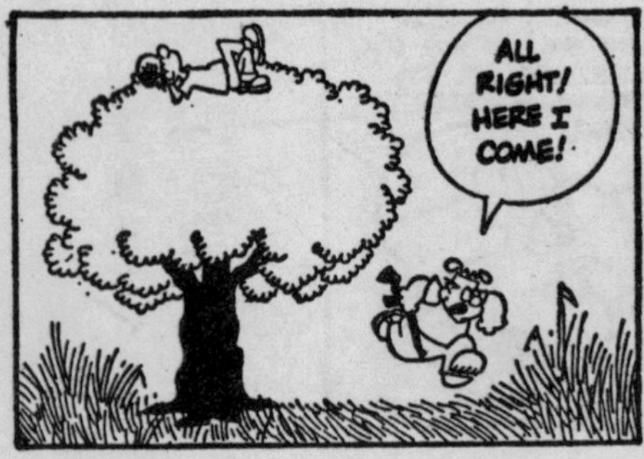
ALL RIGHT! HERE I COME!

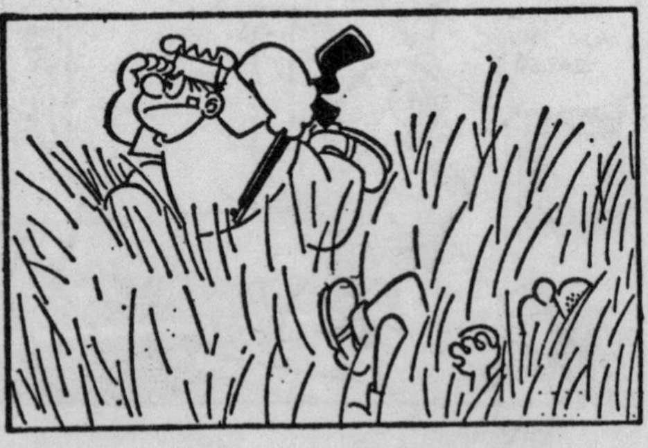

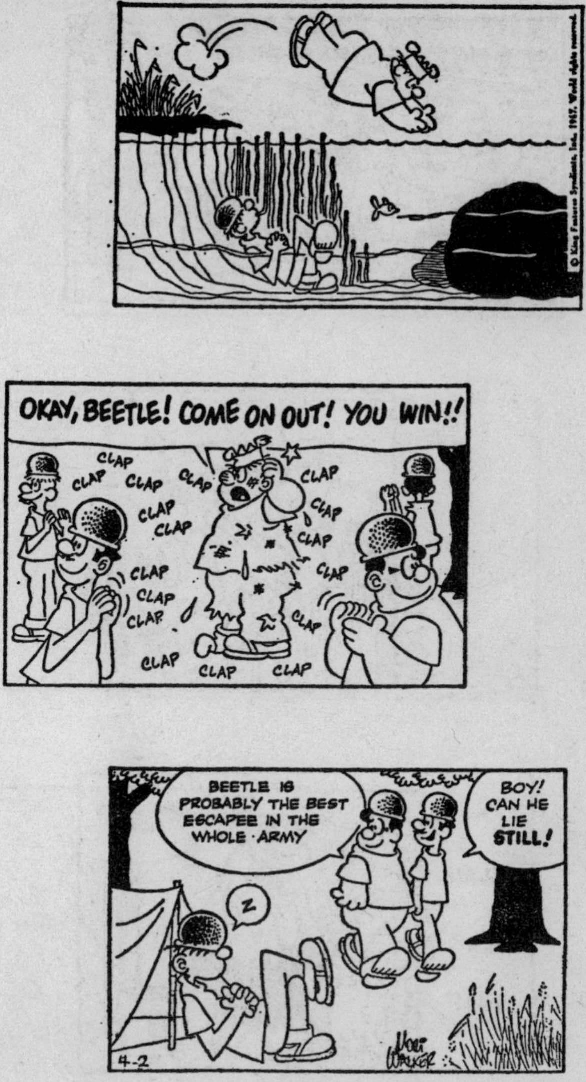
© King Features Syndicate, Inc., 1967. World rights reserved.
OKAY, BEETLE! COME ON OUT! YOU WIN!!
CLAP CLAP CLAP CLAP CLAP CLAP CLAP CLAP CLAP CLAP CLAP CLAP CLAP CLAP CLAP CLAP CLAP
BEETLE IS PROBABLY THE BEST ESCAPEE IN THE WHOLE · ARMY
BOY! CAN HE LIE STILL!
Z
4-2
MORT WALKER

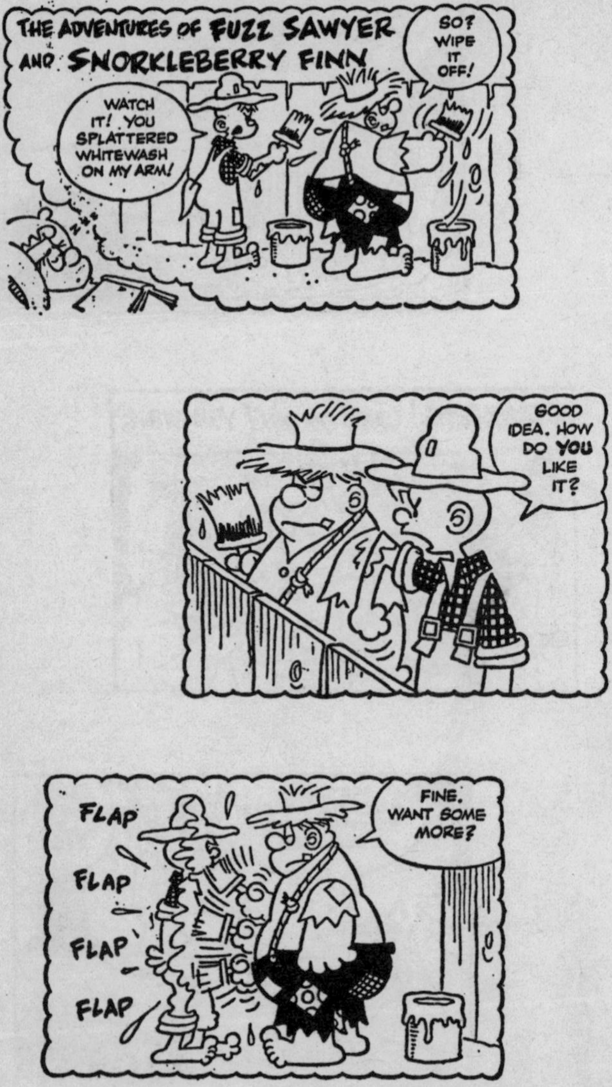
THE ADVENTURES OF FUZZ SAWYER AND SNORKLEBERRY FINN
WATCH IT! YOU SPLATTERED WHITEWASH ON MY ARM!
SO? WIPE IT OFF!
GOOD IDEA. HOW DO YOU LIKE IT?
FLAP
FLAP
FLAP
FLAP
FINE. WANT SOME MORE?

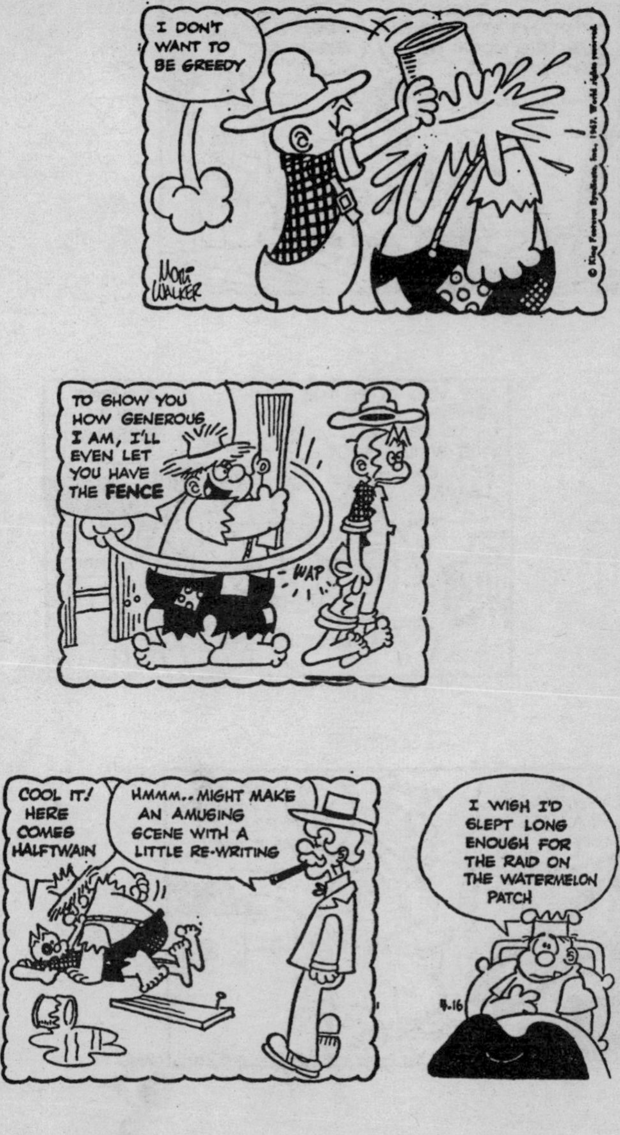
I DON'T WANT TO BE GREEDY
MORT WALKER
© King Features Syndicate, Inc., 1967. World rights reserved.
TO SHOW YOU HOW GENEROUS I AM, I'LL EVEN LET YOU HAVE THE **FENCE**
WAP
COOL IT! HERE COMES HALFTWAIN
HMMM.. MIGHT MAKE AN AMUSING SCENE WITH A LITTLE RE-WRITING
I WISH I'D SLEPT LONG ENOUGH FOR THE RAID ON THE WATERMELON PATCH
8.16

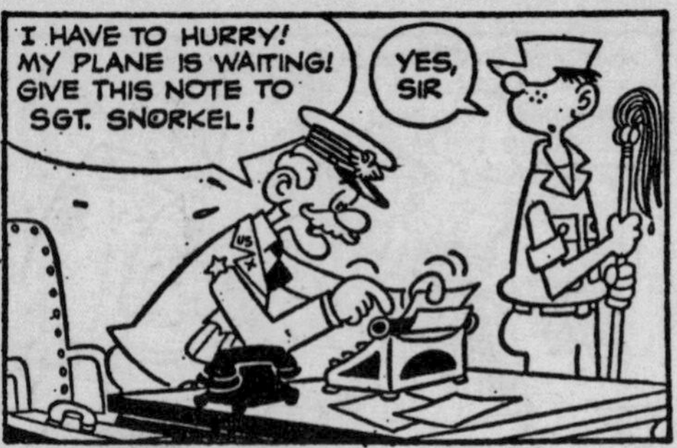
I HAVE TO HURRY! MY PLANE IS WAITING! GIVE THIS NOTE TO SGT. SNORKEL!
YES, SIR

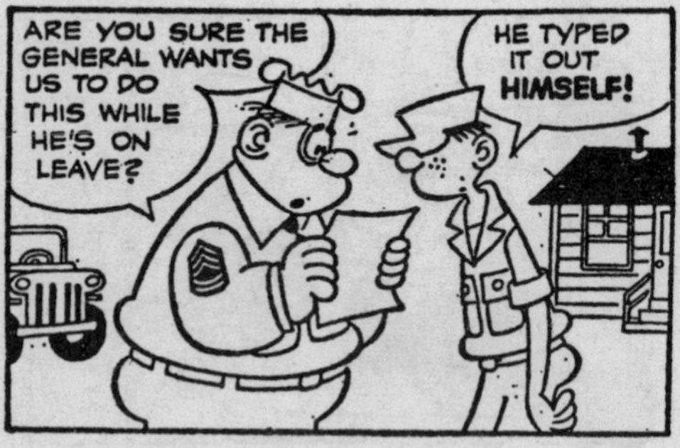
ARE YOU SURE THE GENERAL WANTS US TO DO THIS WHILE HE'S ON LEAVE?
HE TYPED IT OUT HIMSELF!

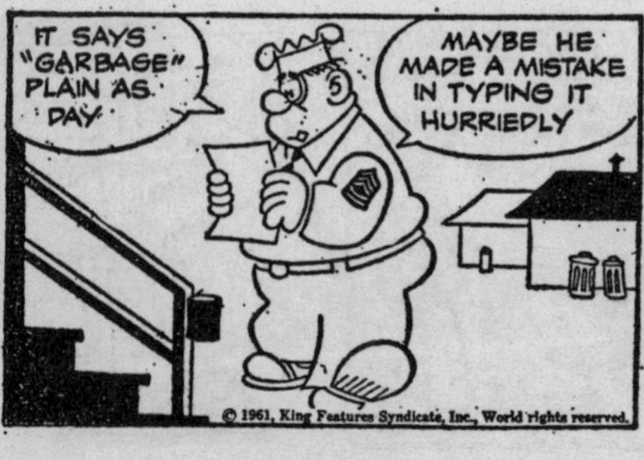
IT SAYS "GARBAGE" PLAIN AS DAY
MAYBE HE MADE A MISTAKE IN TYPING IT HURRIEDLY

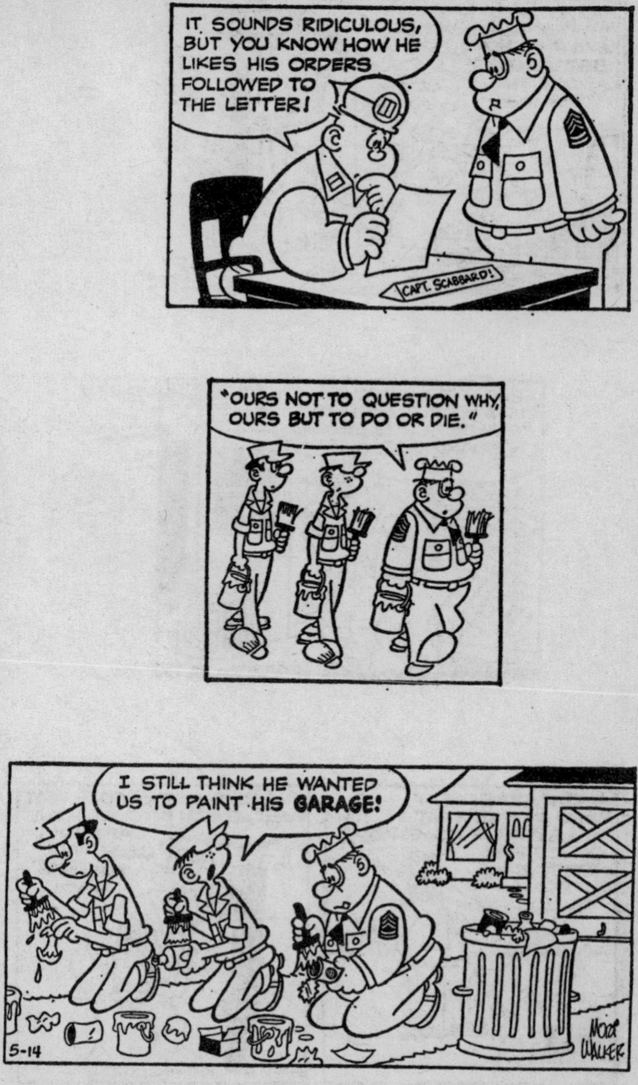
IT SOUNDS RIDICULOUS, BUT YOU KNOW HOW HE LIKES HIS ORDERS FOLLOWED TO THE LETTER!
CAPT. SCABBARD!
"OURS NOT TO QUESTION WHY, OURS BUT TO DO OR DIE."
I STILL THINK HE WANTED US TO PAINT HIS GARAGE!
5-14
MORT WALKER

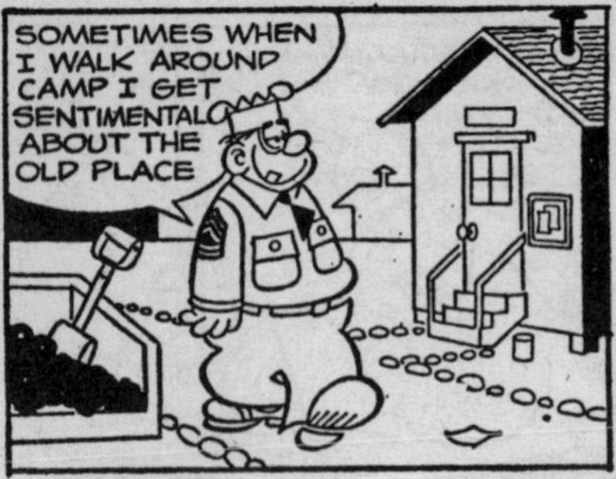
SOMETIMES WHEN I WALK AROUND CAMP I GET SENTIMENTAL ABOUT THE OLD PLACE

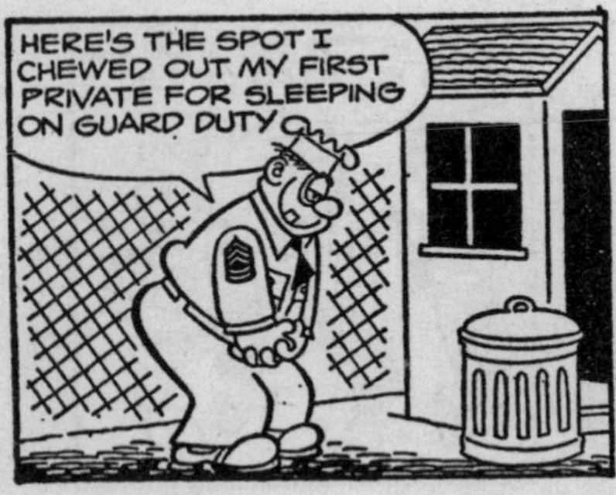
HERE'S THE SPOT I CHEWED OUT MY FIRST PRIVATE FOR SLEEPING ON GUARD DUTY

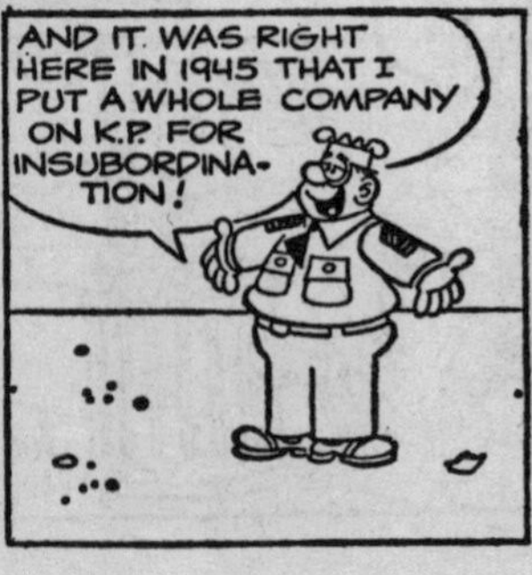
AND IT WAS RIGHT HERE IN 1945 THAT I PUT A WHOLE COMPANY ON K.P. FOR INSUBORDINA-TION!

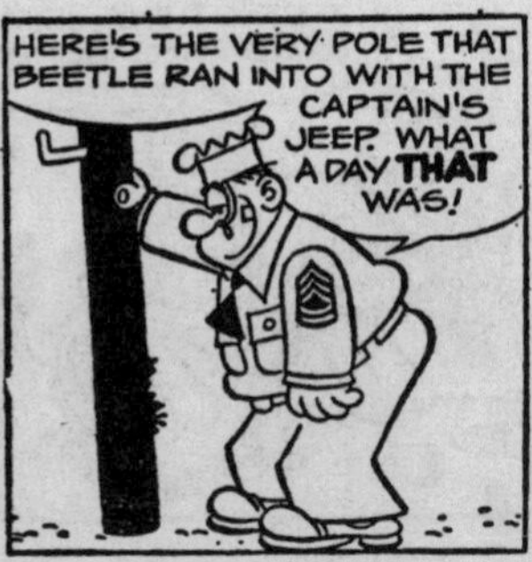
HERE'S THE VERY POLE THAT BEETLE RAN INTO WITH THE CAPTAIN'S JEEP. WHAT A DAY THAT WAS!

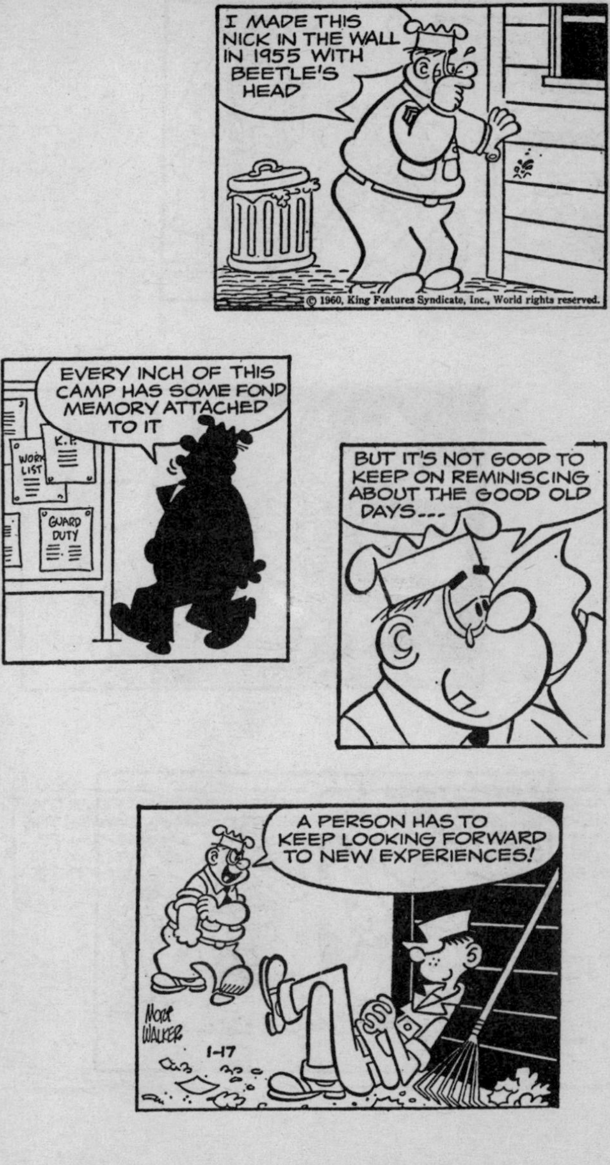
I MADE THIS NICK IN THE WALL IN 1955 WITH BEETLE'S HEAD
© 1960, King Features Syndicate, Inc., World rights reserved.
EVERY INCH OF THIS CAMP HAS SOME FOND MEMORY ATTACHED TO IT
WORK LIST
K.P.
GUARD DUTY
BUT IT'S NOT GOOD TO KEEP ON REMINISCING ABOUT THE GOOD OLD DAYS...
A PERSON HAS TO KEEP LOOKING FORWARD TO NEW EXPERIENCES!
MORT WALKER
1-17

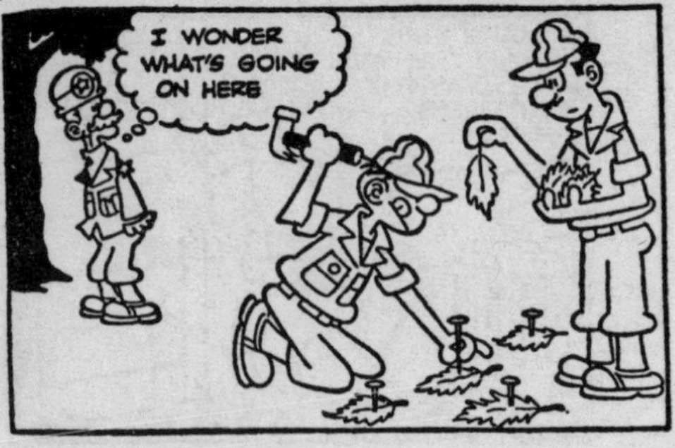
I WONDER WHAT'S GOING ON HERE

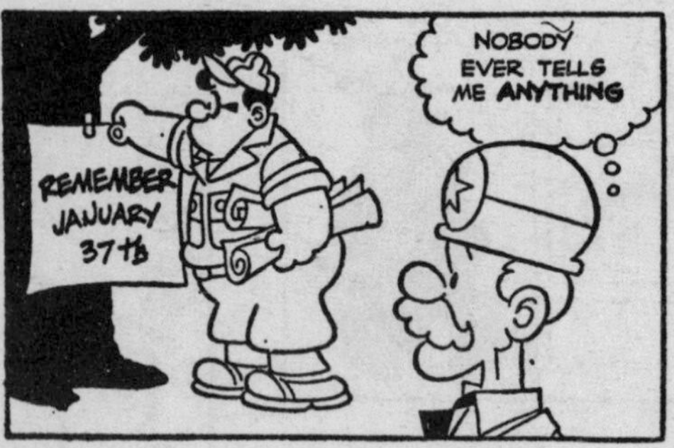
REMEMBER JANUARY 37⅓
NOBODY EVER TELLS ME ANYTHING

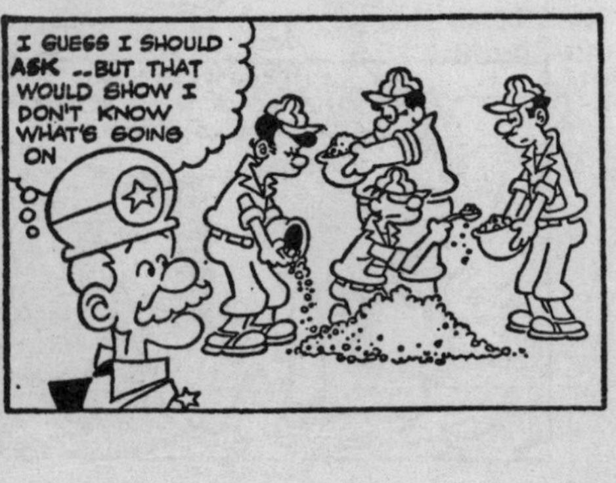
I GUESS I SHOULD ASK --BUT THAT WOULD SHOW I DON'T KNOW WHAT'S GOING ON

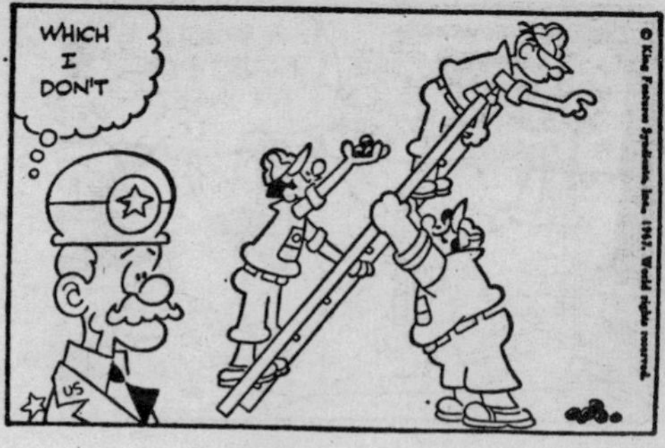
WHICH I DON'T
© King Features Syndicate, Inc., 1967. World rights reserved.

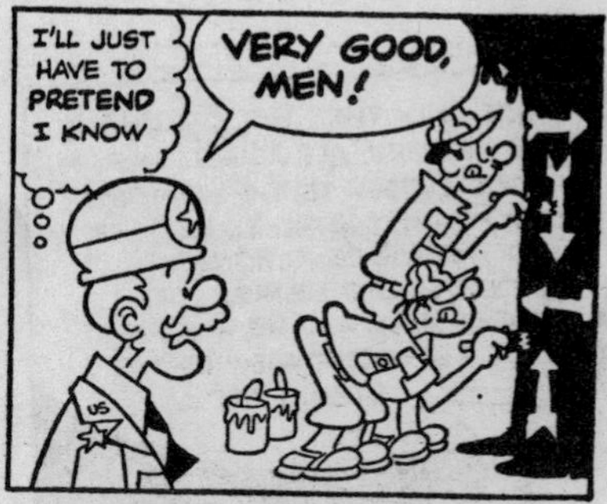
I'LL JUST HAVE TO PRETEND I KNOW
VERY GOOD, MEN!

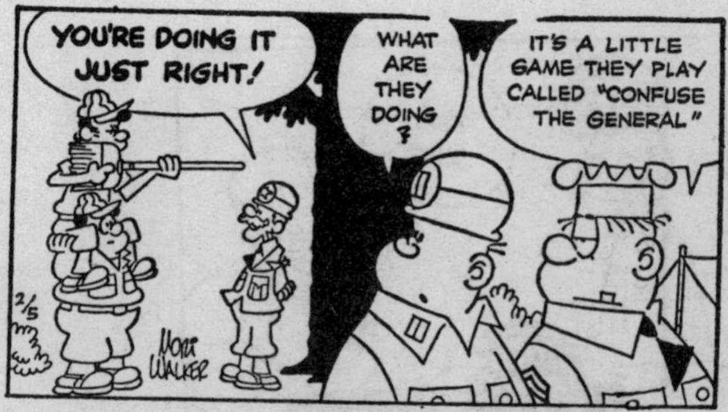
YOU'RE DOING IT JUST RIGHT!
WHAT ARE THEY DOING?
IT'S A LITTLE GAME THEY PLAY CALLED "CONFUSE THE GENERAL"
2/5
MORT WALKER

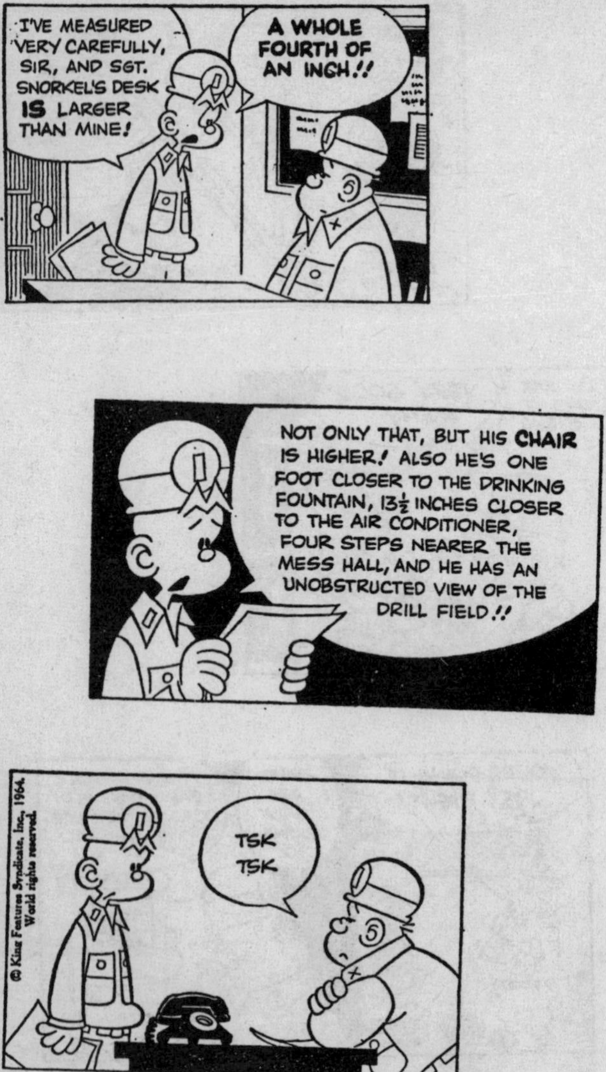

I'VE MEASURED VERY CAREFULLY, SIR, AND SGT. SNORKEL'S DESK **IS** LARGER THAN MINE!
A WHOLE FOURTH OF AN INCH!!
NOT ONLY THAT, BUT HIS **CHAIR** IS HIGHER! ALSO HE'S ONE FOOT CLOSER TO THE DRINKING FOUNTAIN, $13\frac{1}{2}$ INCHES CLOSER TO THE AIR CONDITIONER, FOUR STEPS NEARER THE MESS HALL, AND HE HAS AN UNOBSTRUCTED VIEW OF THE DRILL FIELD!!
TSK TSK
© King Features Syndicate, Inc., 1964. World rights reserved.

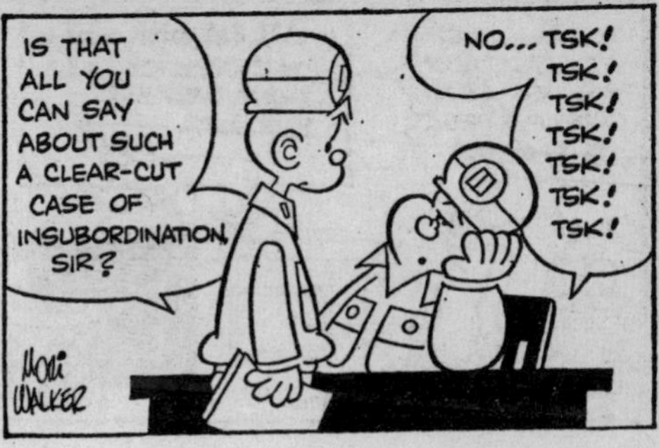
IS THAT ALL YOU CAN SAY ABOUT SUCH A CLEAR-CUT CASE OF INSUBORDINATION, SIR?
NO... TSK! TSK! TSK! TSK! TSK! TSK! TSK!
MORT WALKER

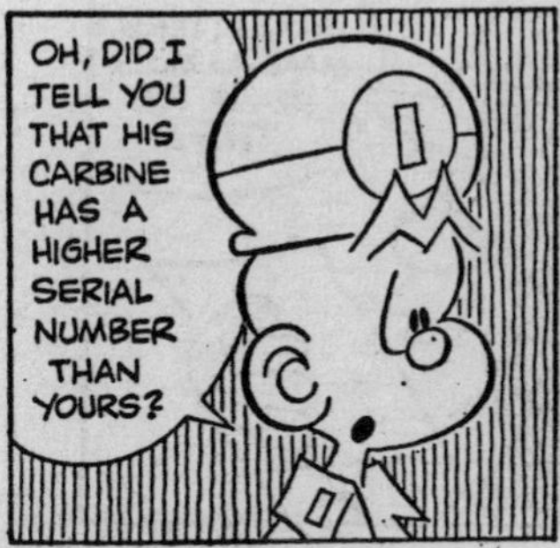
OH, DID I TELL YOU THAT HIS CARBINE HAS A HIGHER SERIAL NUMBER THAN YOURS?

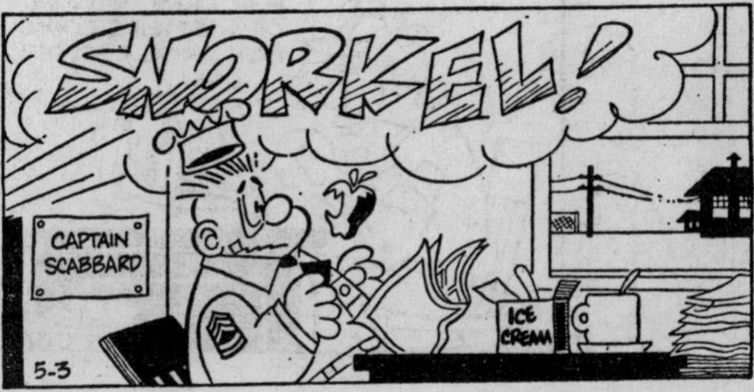
SNORKEL!
CAPTAIN SCABBARD
ICE CREAM
5-3

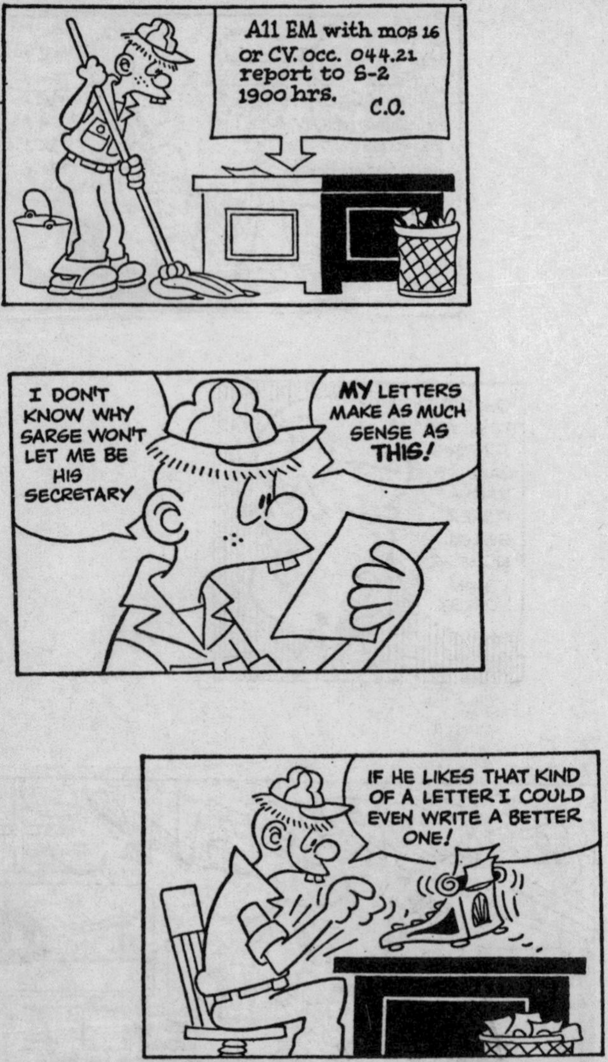
All EM with mos 16 or CV. occ. 044.21 report to S-2 1900 hrs. C.O.
I DON'T KNOW WHY SARGE WON'T LET ME BE HIS SECRETARY
MY LETTERS MAKE AS MUCH SENSE AS THIS!
IF HE LIKES THAT KIND OF A LETTER I COULD EVEN WRITE A BETTER ONE!

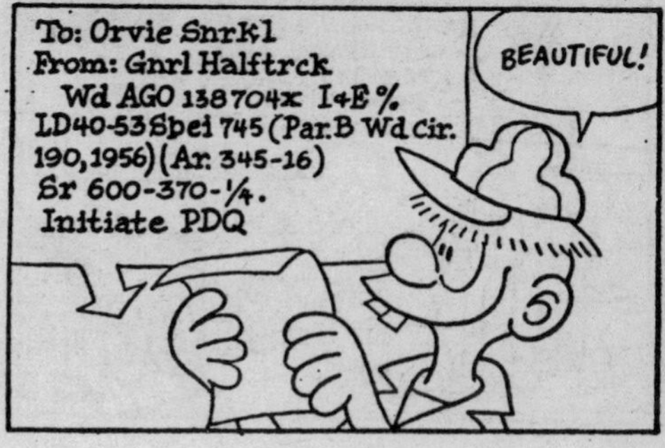
To: Orvie Snrkl
From: Gnrl Halftrck
Wd AGO 138704x I4E %
LD40-53 Spel 745 (Par. B Wd Cir. 190, 1956) (Ar. 345-16)
Sr 600-370-¼.
Initiate PDQ
BEAUTIFUL!

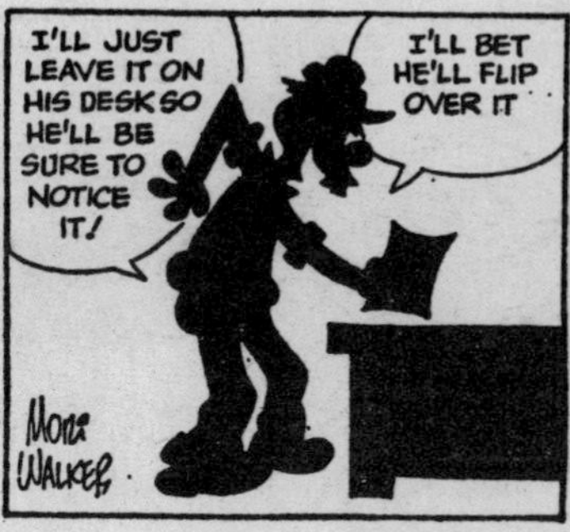
I'LL JUST LEAVE IT ON HIS DESK SO HE'LL BE SURE TO NOTICE IT!
I'LL BET HE'LL FLIP OVER IT
MORT WALKER

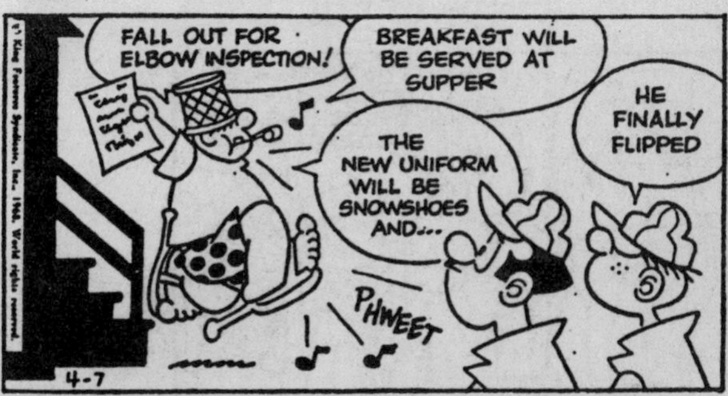
FALL OUT FOR ELBOW INSPECTION!
BREAKFAST WILL BE SERVED AT SUPPER
THE NEW UNIFORM WILL BE SNOWSHOES AND...
HE FINALLY FLIPPED
PHWEET
4-7
© King Features Syndicate, Inc., 1968. World rights reserved.

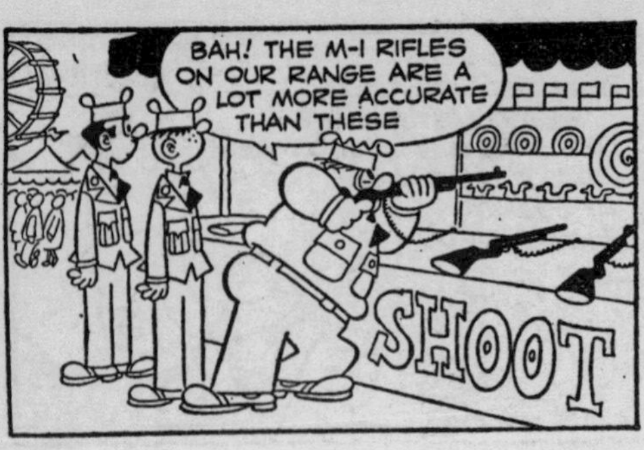
BAH! THE M-1 RIFLES ON OUR RANGE ARE A LOT MORE ACCURATE THAN THESE
SHOOT

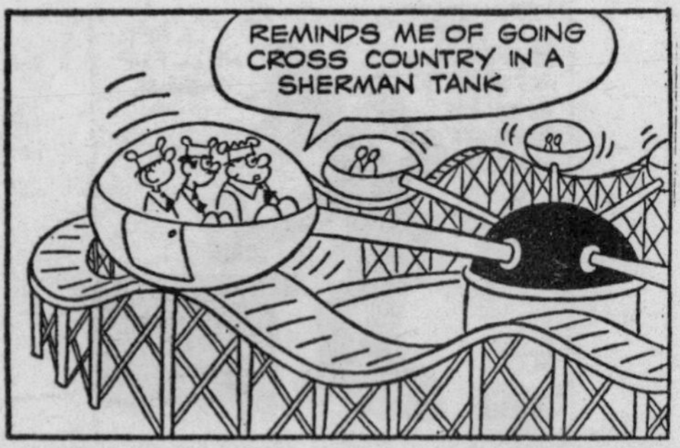
REMINDS ME OF GOING CROSS COUNTRY IN A SHERMAN TANK

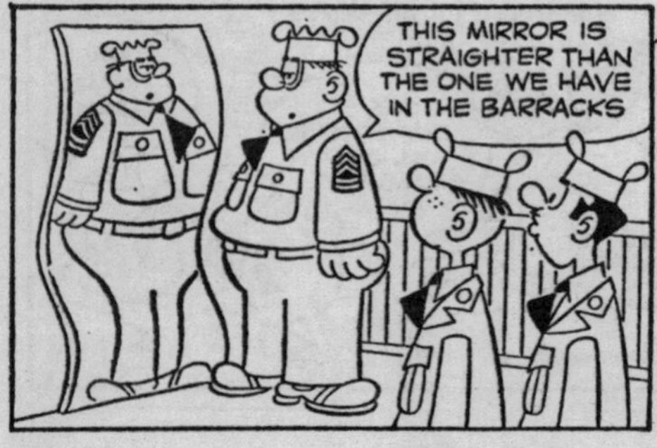
THIS MIRROR IS STRAIGHTER THAN THE ONE WE HAVE IN THE BARRACKS

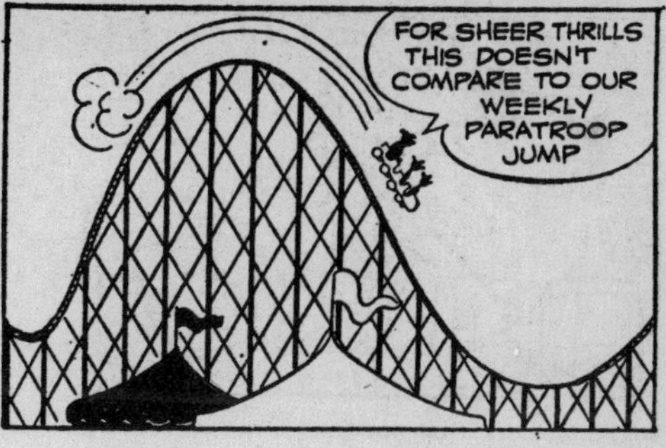
FOR SHEER THRILLS THIS DOESN'T COMPARE TO OUR WEEKLY PARATROOP JUMP

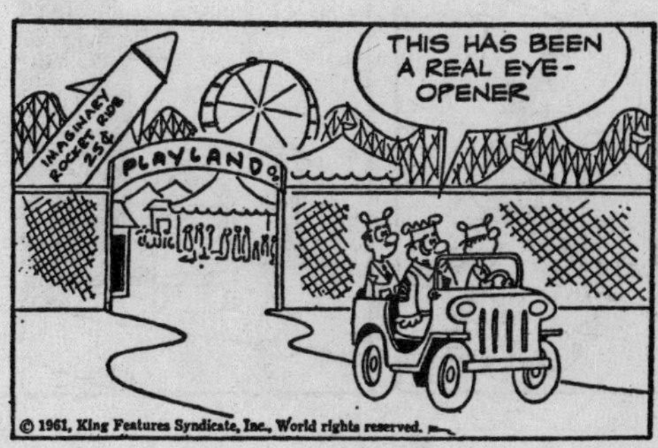
THIS HAS BEEN A REAL EYE-OPENER
IMAGINARY ROCKET RIDE 25¢
PLAYLAND
© 1961, King Features Syndicate, Inc., World rights reserved.

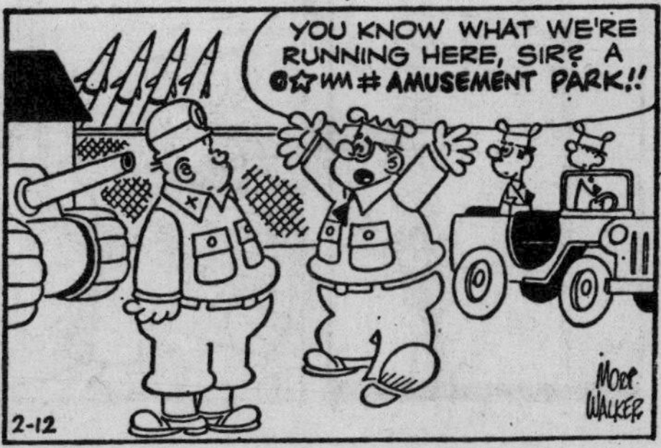
YOU KNOW WHAT WE'RE RUNNING HERE, SIR? A @☆WM # AMUSEMENT PARK!!
2-12
MORT WALKER

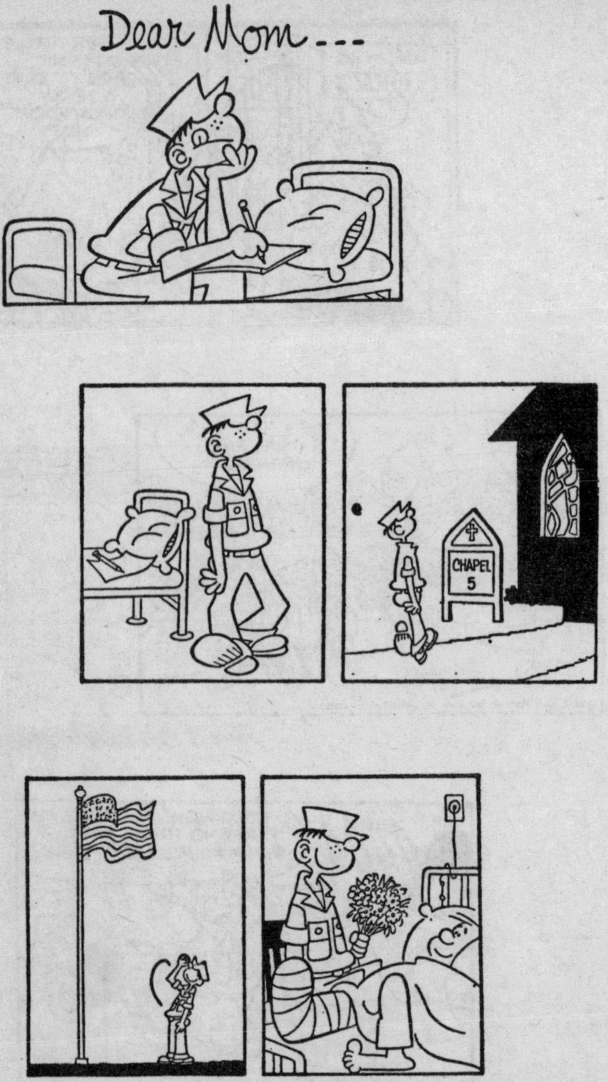
Dear Mom...
CHAPEL
5

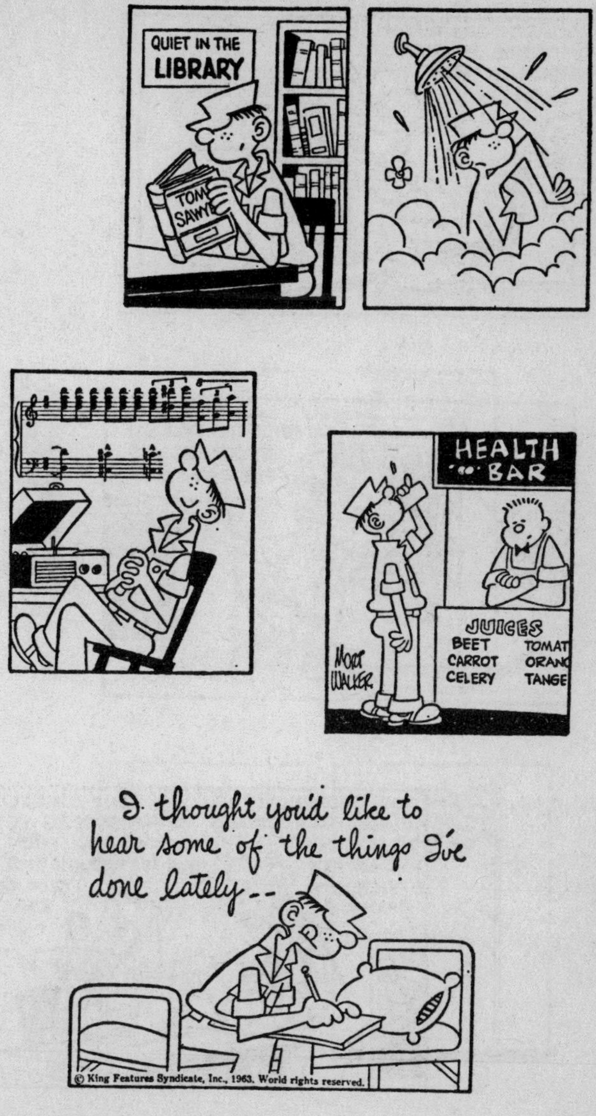
QUIET IN THE LIBRARY
TOM SAWY
HEALTH BAR
JUICES
BEET
CARROT
CELERY
TOMAT
ORAN
TANGE
MORT WALKER
I thought you'd like to hear some of the things I've done lately--
© King Features Syndicate, Inc., 1963. World rights reserved.

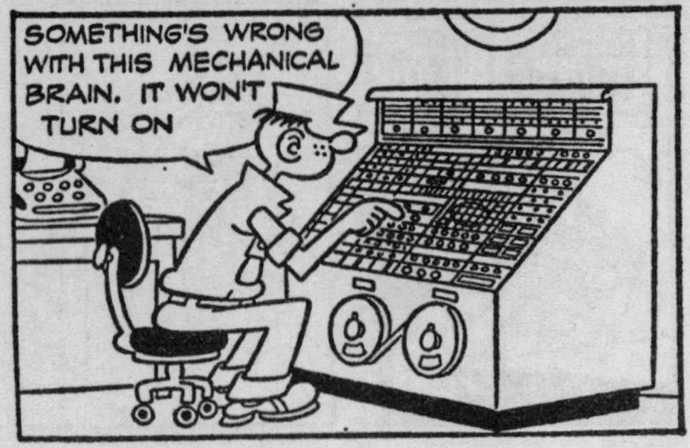
SOMETHING'S WRONG WITH THIS MECHANICAL BRAIN. IT WON'T TURN ON

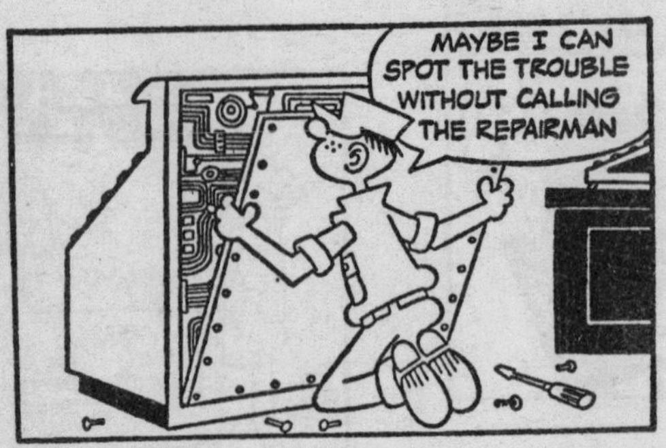
MAYBE I CAN SPOT THE TROUBLE WITHOUT CALLING THE REPAIRMAN

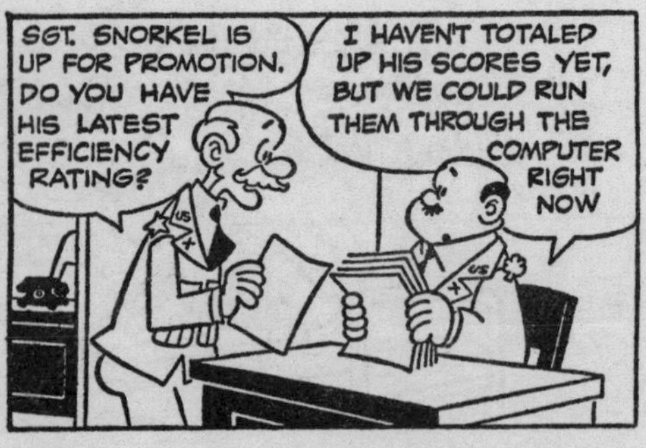
SGT. SNORKEL IS UP FOR PROMOTION. DO YOU HAVE HIS LATEST EFFICIENCY RATING?
I HAVEN'T TOTALED UP HIS SCORES YET, BUT WE COULD RUN THEM THROUGH THE COMPUTER RIGHT NOW

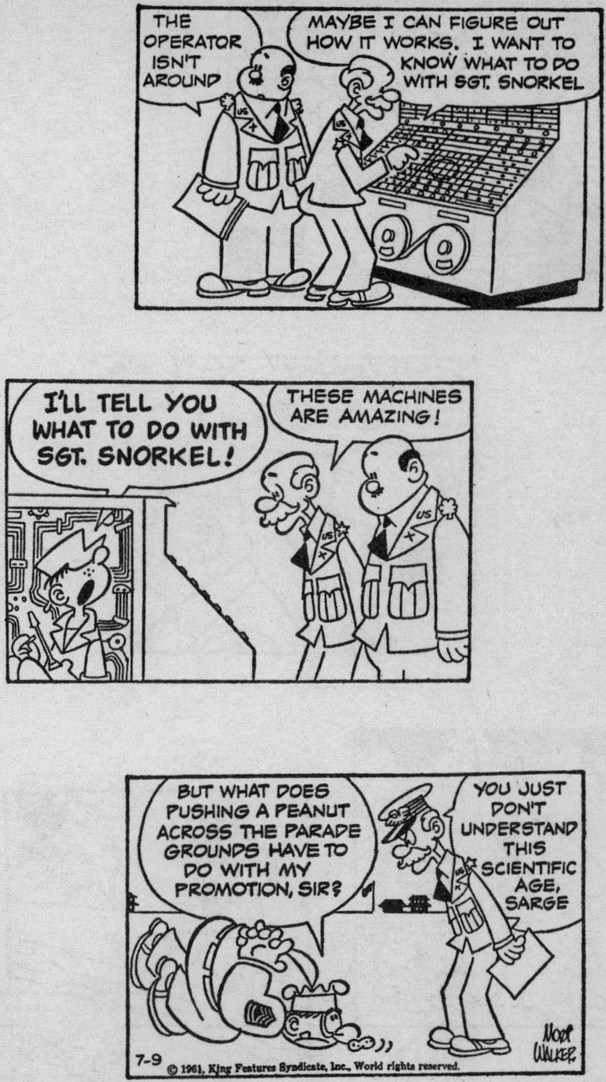
THE OPERATOR ISN'T AROUND
MAYBE I CAN FIGURE OUT HOW IT WORKS. I WANT TO KNOW WHAT TO DO WITH SGT. SNORKEL
I'LL TELL YOU WHAT TO DO WITH SGT. SNORKEL!
THESE MACHINES ARE AMAZING!
BUT WHAT DOES PUSHING A PEANUT ACROSS THE PARADE GROUNDS HAVE TO DO WITH MY PROMOTION, SIR?
YOU JUST DON'T UNDERSTAND THIS SCIENTIFIC AGE, SARGE
7-9
MORT WALKER

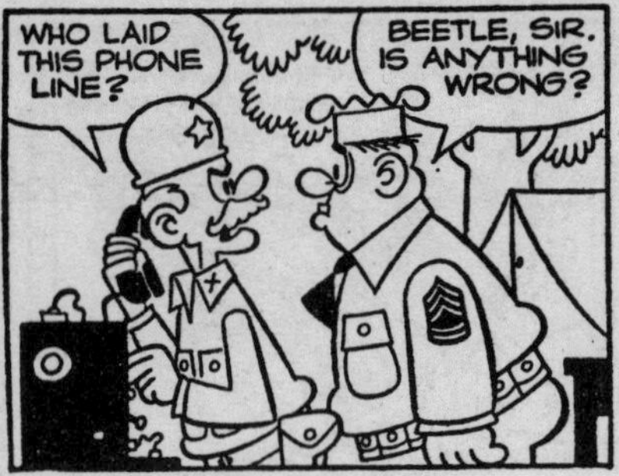
WHO LAID THIS PHONE LINE?
BEETLE, SIR. IS ANYTHING WRONG?

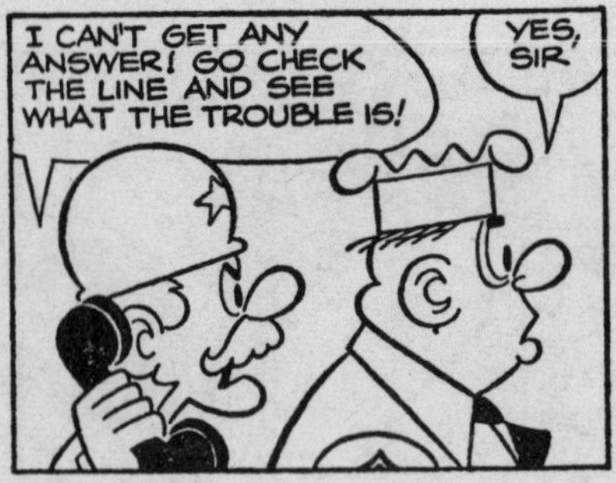
I CAN'T GET ANY ANSWER! GO CHECK THE LINE AND SEE WHAT THE TROUBLE IS!
YES, SIR

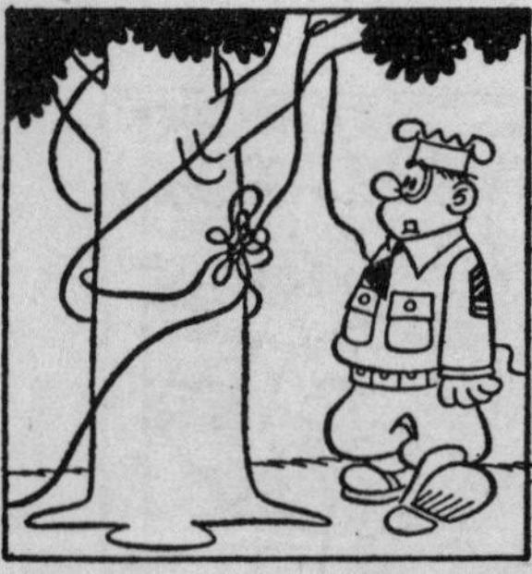

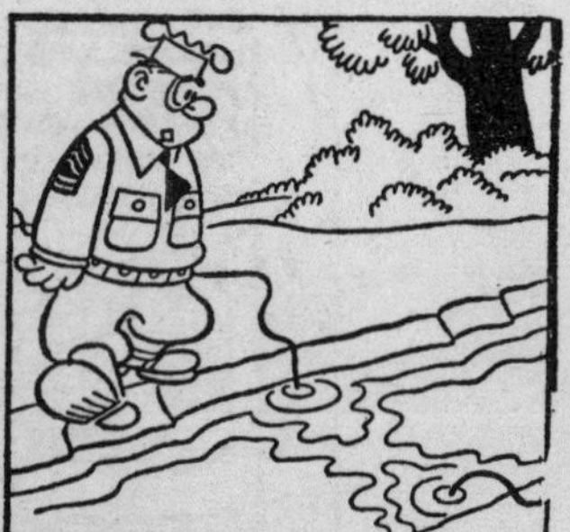

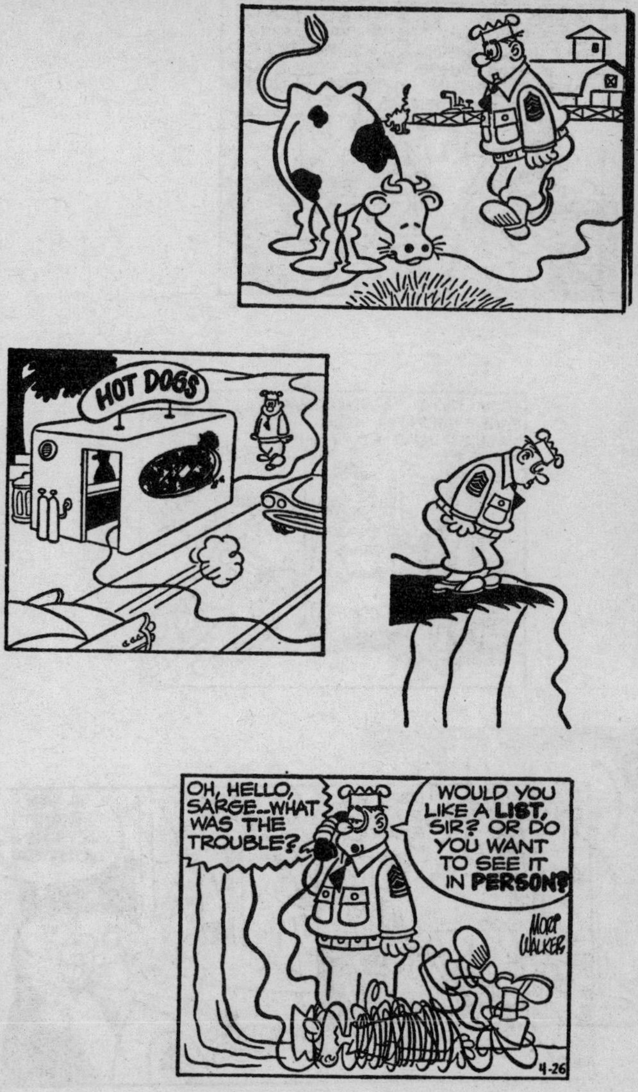
HOT DOGS
OH, HELLO, SARGE..WHAT WAS THE TROUBLE?
WOULD YOU LIKE A **LIST,** SIR? OR DO YOU WANT TO SEE IT IN **PERSON?**
MORT WALKER
4-26

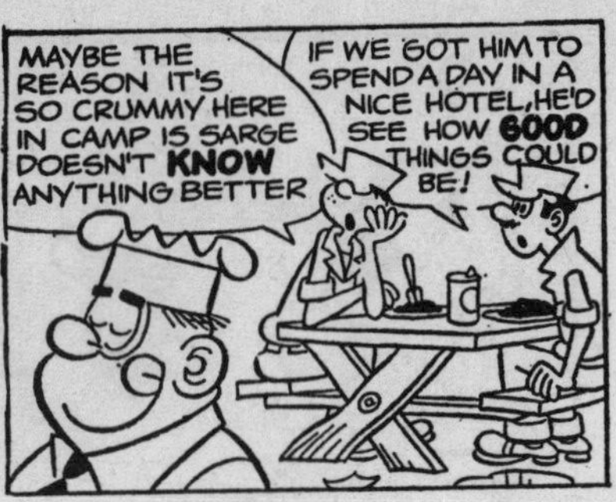
MAYBE THE REASON IT'S SO CRUMMY HERE IN CAMP IS SARGE DOESN'T **KNOW** ANYTHING BETTER
IF WE GOT HIM TO SPEND A DAY IN A NICE HOTEL, HE'D SEE HOW **GOOD** THINGS COULD BE!

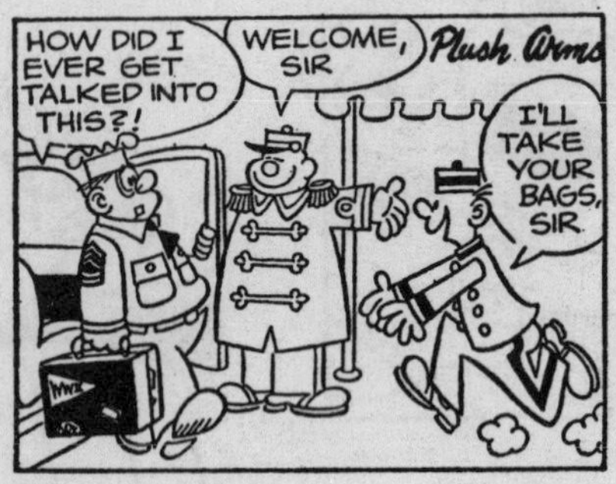
HOW DID I EVER GET TALKED INTO THIS?!
WELCOME, SIR
Plush Arms
I'LL TAKE YOUR BAGS, SIR.

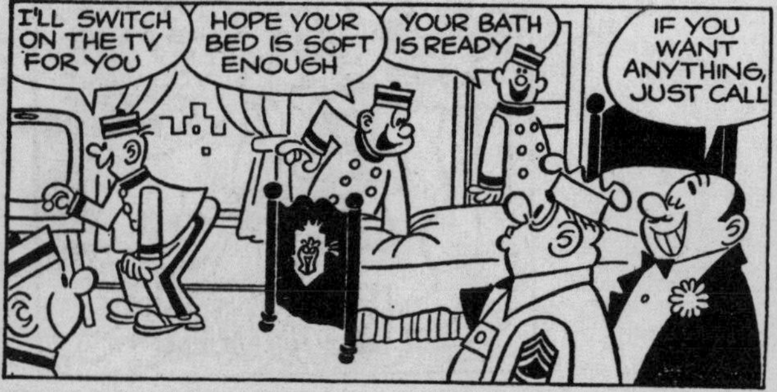
I'LL SWITCH ON THE TV FOR YOU
HOPE YOUR BED IS SOFT ENOUGH
YOUR BATH IS READY
IF YOU WANT ANYTHING, JUST CALL

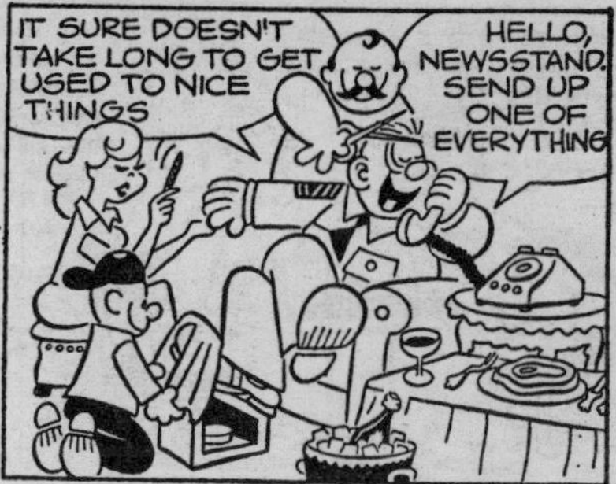
IT SURE DOESN'T TAKE LONG TO GET USED TO NICE THINGS
HELLO, NEWSSTAND. SEND UP ONE OF EVERYTHING

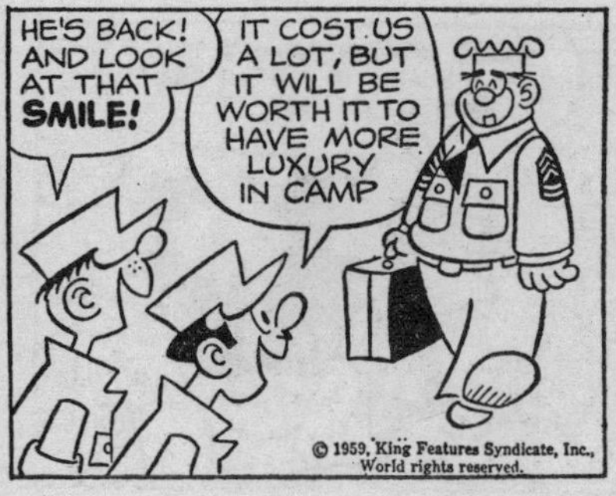
HE'S BACK! AND LOOK AT THAT **SMILE!**
IT COST US A LOT, BUT IT WILL BE WORTH IT TO HAVE MORE LUXURY IN CAMP

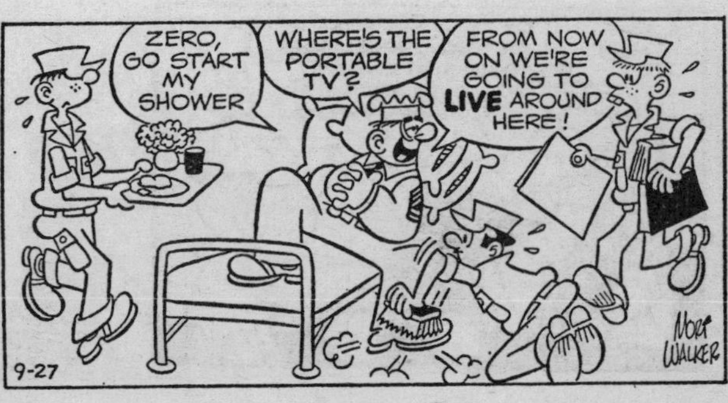
ZERO, GO START MY SHOWER
WHERE'S THE PORTABLE TV?
FROM NOW ON WE'RE GOING TO **LIVE** AROUND HERE!
MORT WALKER
9-27

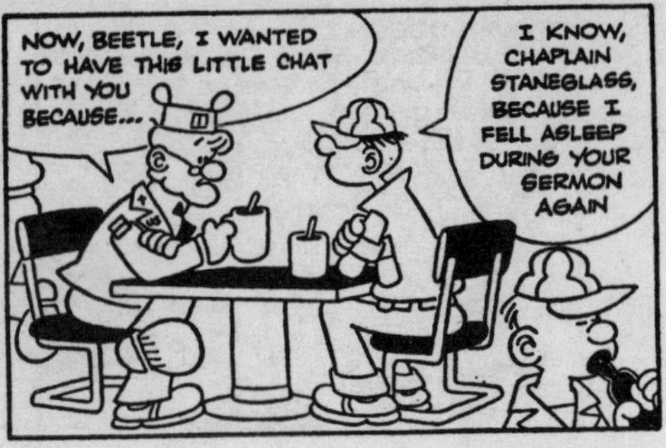
NOW, BEETLE, I WANTED TO HAVE THIS LITTLE CHAT WITH YOU BECAUSE...
I KNOW, CHAPLAIN STANEGLASS, BECAUSE I FELL ASLEEP DURING YOUR SERMON AGAIN

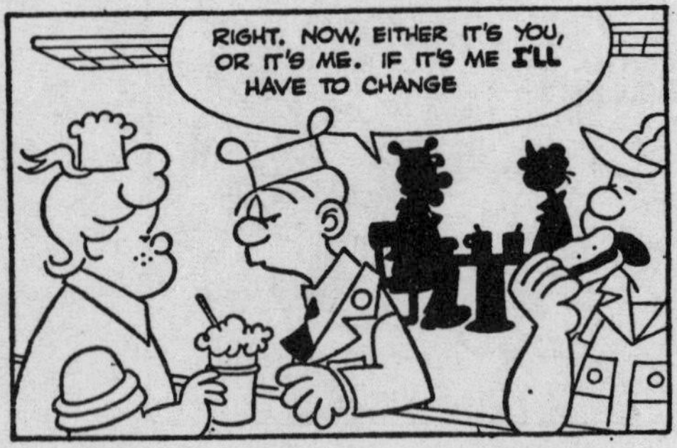
RIGHT. NOW, EITHER IT'S YOU, OR IT'S ME. IF IT'S ME **I'LL** HAVE TO CHANGE

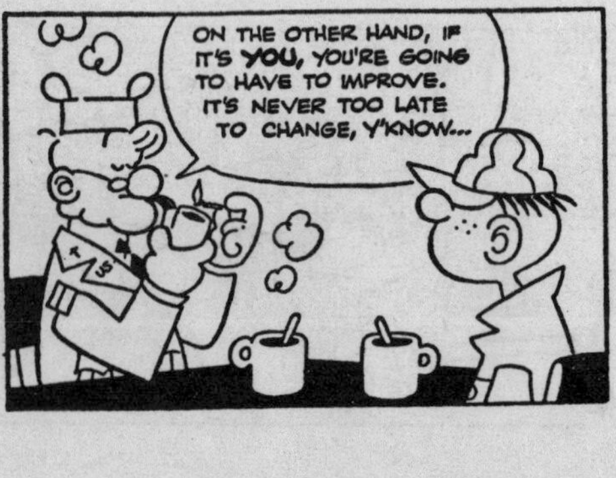
ON THE OTHER HAND, IF IT'S **YOU,** YOU'RE GOING TO HAVE TO IMPROVE. IT'S NEVER TOO LATE TO CHANGE, Y'KNOW...

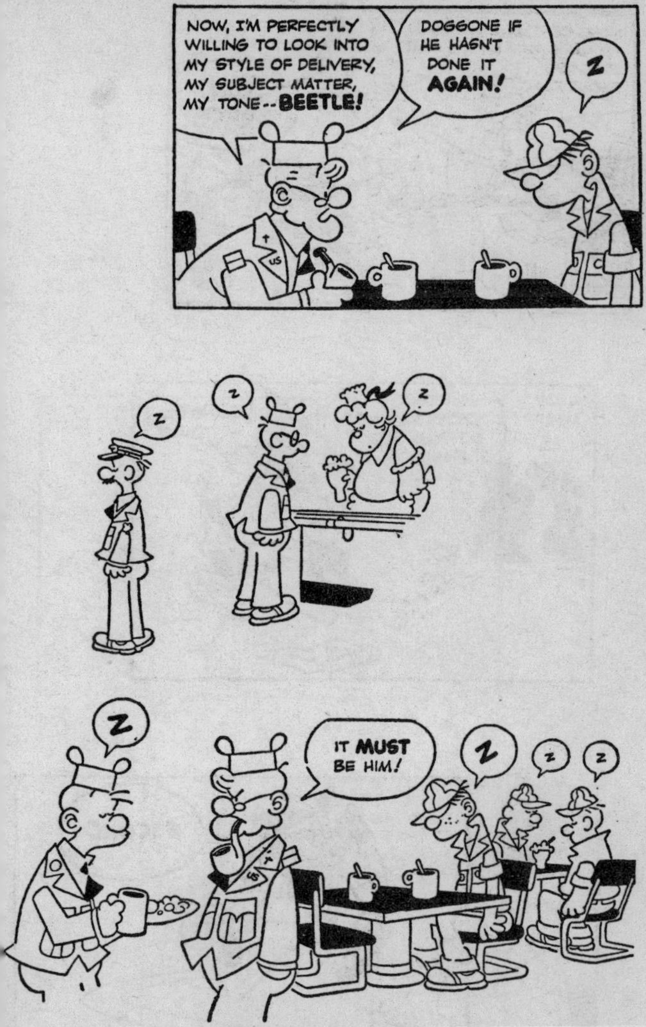
NOW, I'M PERFECTLY WILLING TO LOOK INTO MY STYLE OF DELIVERY, MY SUBJECT MATTER, MY TONE--BEETLE!
DOGGONE IF HE HASN'T DONE IT AGAIN!
Z
Z
Z
Z
Z
IT MUST BE HIM!
Z
Z
Z

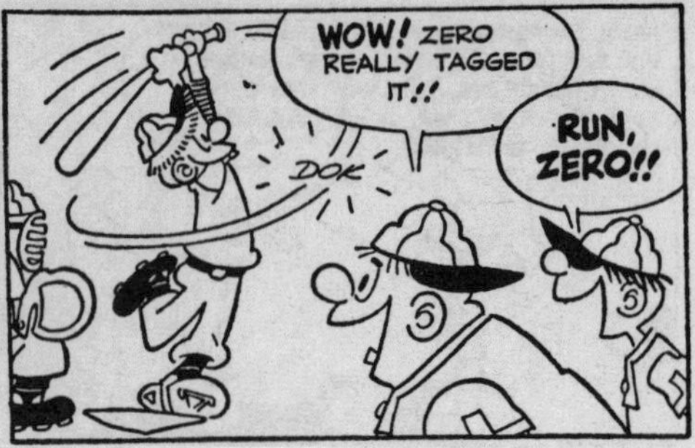
WOW! ZERO REALLY TAGGED IT!!
RUN, ZERO!!
DOK

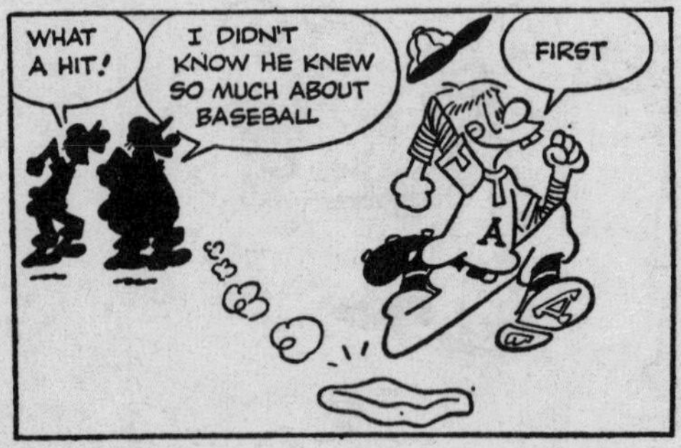
WHAT A HIT!
I DIDN'T KNOW HE KNEW SO MUCH ABOUT BASEBALL
FIRST

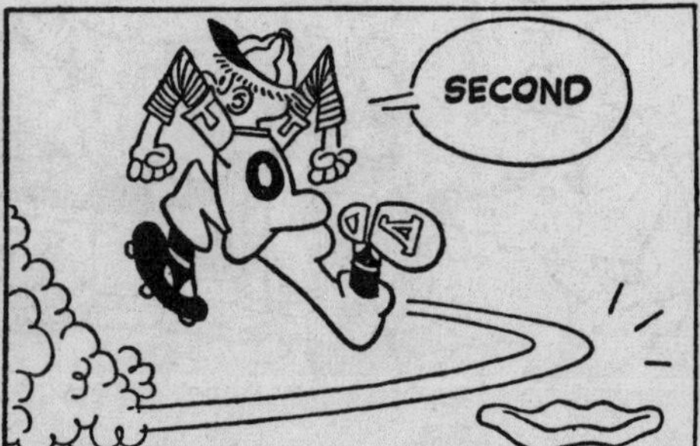
SECOND

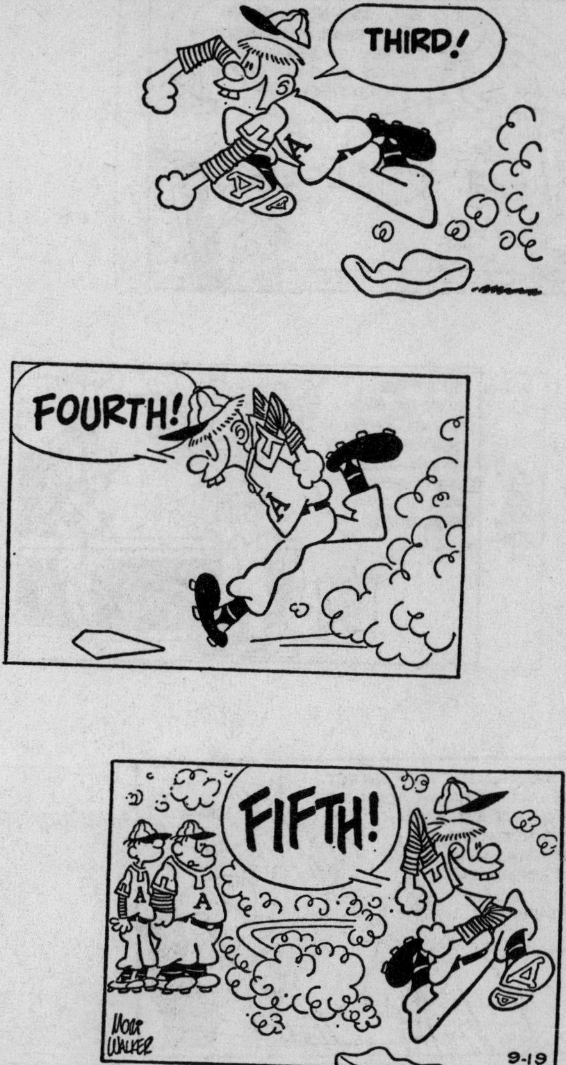
THIRD!
FOURTH!
FIFTH!
MORT WALKER
9-19

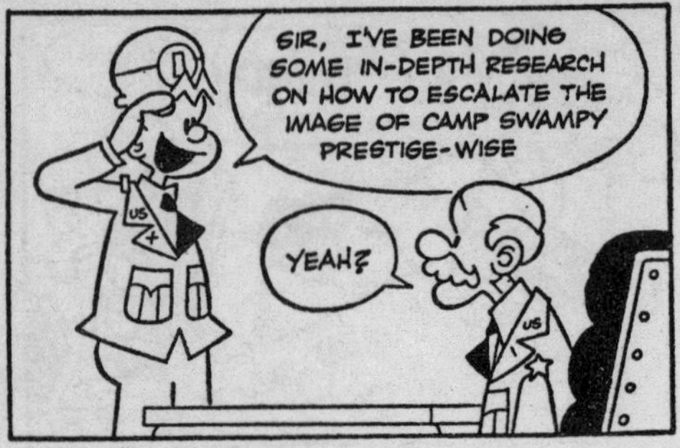
SIR, I'VE BEEN DOING SOME IN-DEPTH RESEARCH ON HOW TO ESCALATE THE IMAGE OF CAMP SWAMPY PRESTIGE-WISE
YEAH?

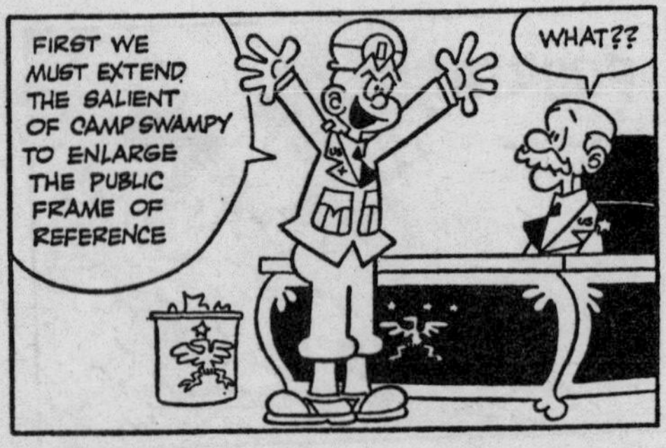
FIRST WE MUST EXTEND THE SALIENT OF CAMP SWAMPY TO ENLARGE THE PUBLIC FRAME OF REFERENCE
WHAT??

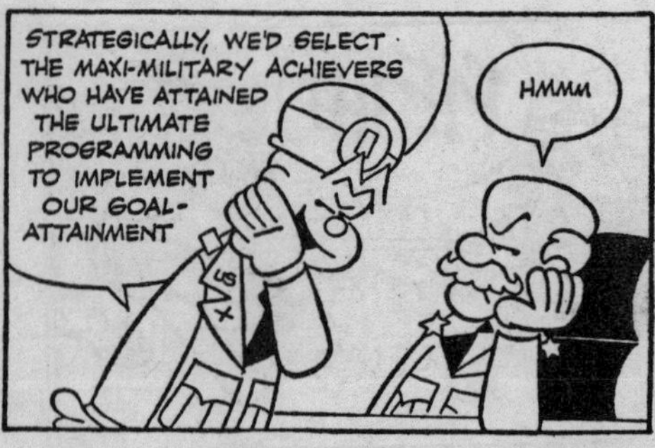
STRATEGICALLY, WE'D SELECT THE MAXI-MILITARY ACHIEVERS WHO HAVE ATTAINED THE ULTIMATE PROGRAMMING TO IMPLEMENT OUR GOAL-ATTAINMENT
HMMM

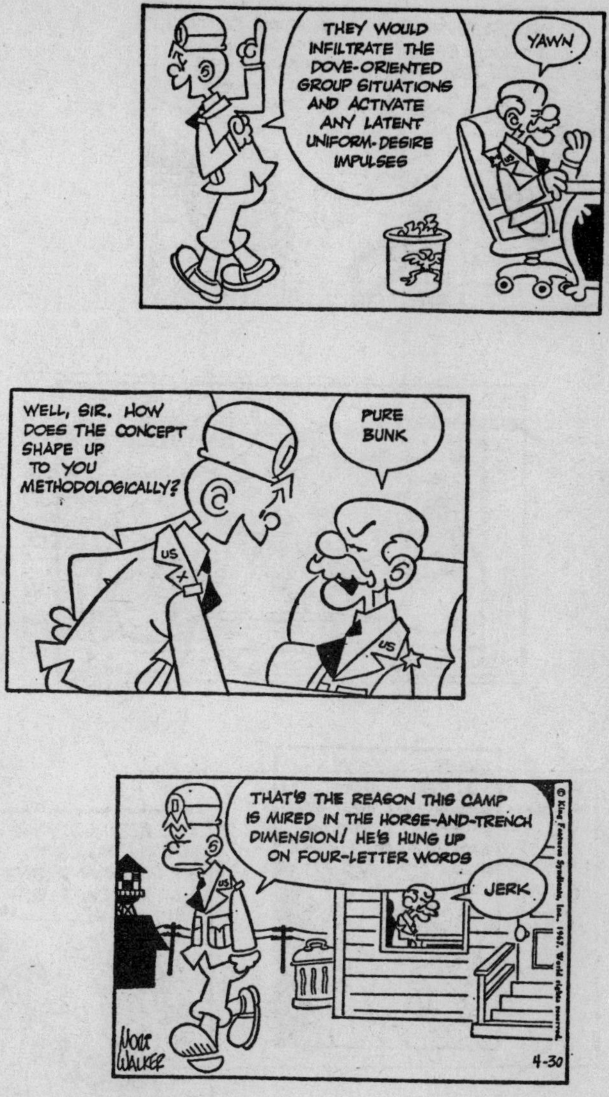
THEY WOULD INFILTRATE THE DOVE-ORIENTED GROUP SITUATIONS AND ACTIVATE ANY LATENT UNIFORM-DESIRE IMPULSES
YAWN
WELL, SIR. HOW DOES THE CONCEPT SHAPE UP TO YOU METHODOLOGICALLY?
PURE BUNK
THAT'S THE REASON THIS CAMP IS MIRED IN THE HORSE-AND-TRENCH DIMENSION! HE'S HUNG UP ON FOUR-LETTER WORDS
JERK
MORT WALKER
4-30
© King Features Syndicate, Inc., 1967. World rights reserved.

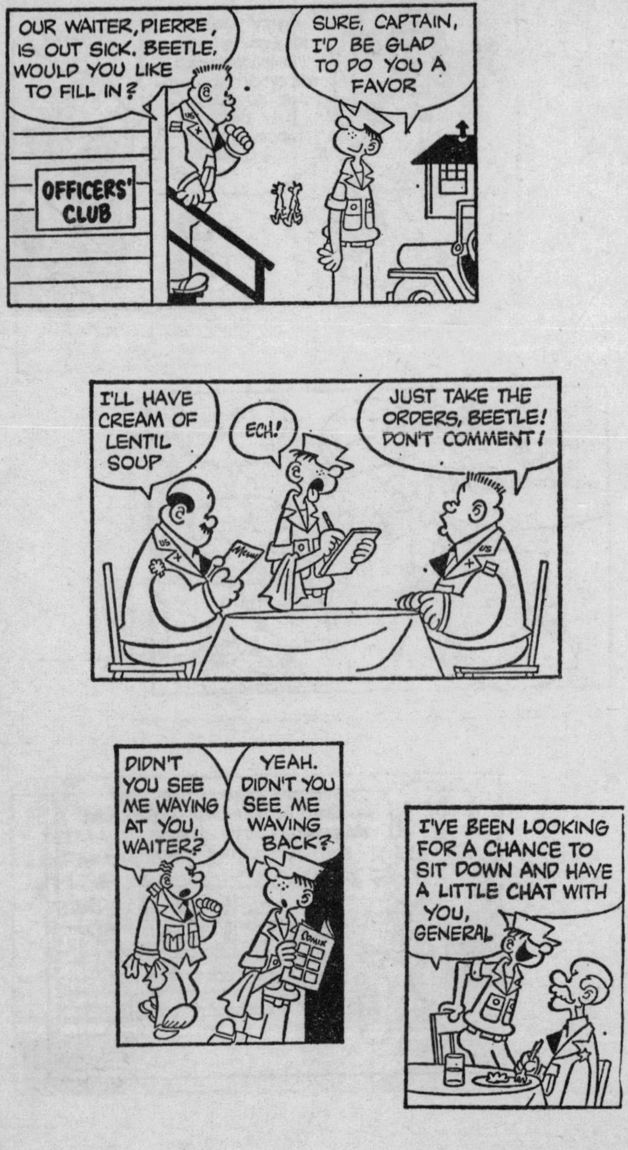
OUR WAITER, PIERRE, IS OUT SICK. BEETLE, WOULD YOU LIKE TO FILL IN?
SURE, CAPTAIN, I'D BE GLAD TO DO YOU A FAVOR
OFFICERS' CLUB
I'LL HAVE CREAM OF LENTIL SOUP
ECH!
JUST TAKE THE ORDERS, BEETLE! DON'T COMMENT!
DIDN'T YOU SEE ME WAVING AT YOU, WAITER?
YEAH. DIDN'T YOU SEE ME WAVING BACK?
COMIX
I'VE BEEN LOOKING FOR A CHANCE TO SIT DOWN AND HAVE A LITTLE CHAT WITH YOU, GENERAL

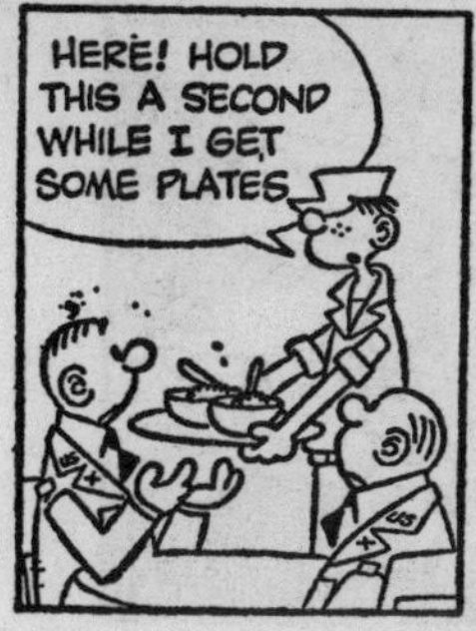
HERE! HOLD THIS A SECOND WHILE I GET SOME PLATES

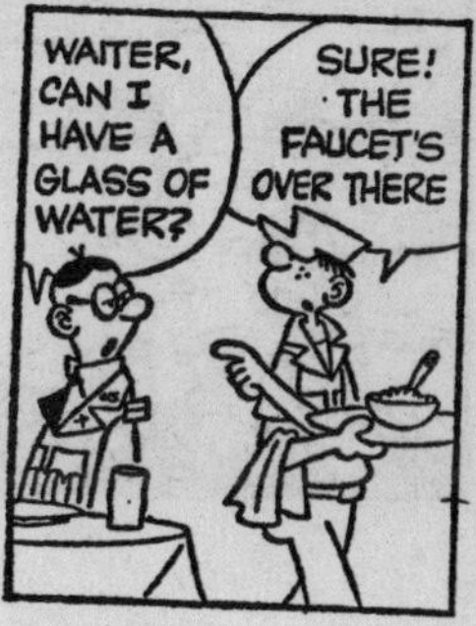
WAITER, CAN I HAVE A GLASS OF WATER?
SURE! THE FAUCET'S OVER THERE

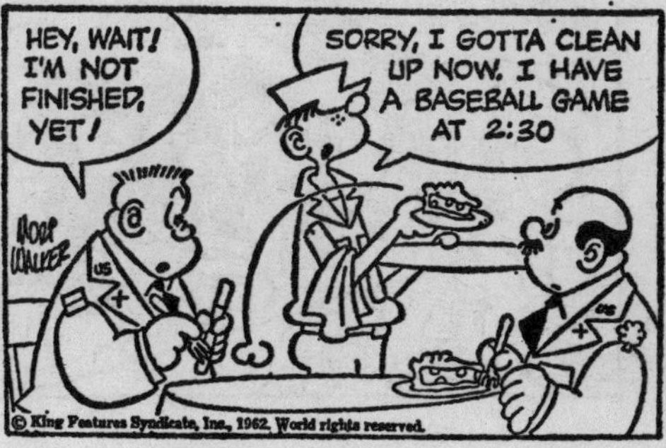
HEY, WAIT! I'M NOT FINISHED, YET!
SORRY, I GOTTA CLEAN UP NOW. I HAVE A BASEBALL GAME AT 2:30
MORT WALKER
© King Features Syndicate, Inc., 1962. World rights reserved.

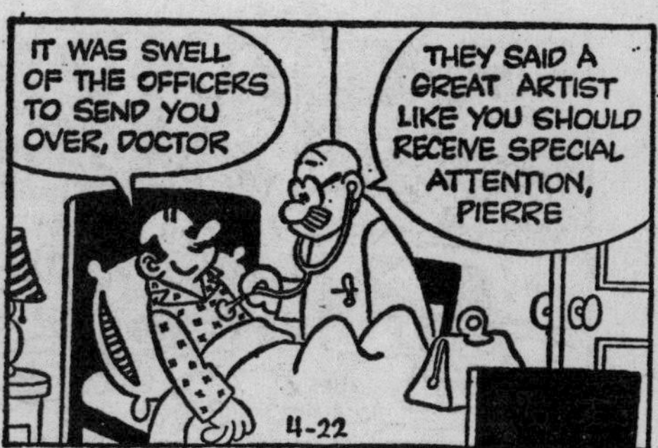
IT WAS SWELL OF THE OFFICERS TO SEND YOU OVER, DOCTOR
THEY SAID A GREAT ARTIST LIKE YOU SHOULD RECEIVE SPECIAL ATTENTION, PIERRE
4-22

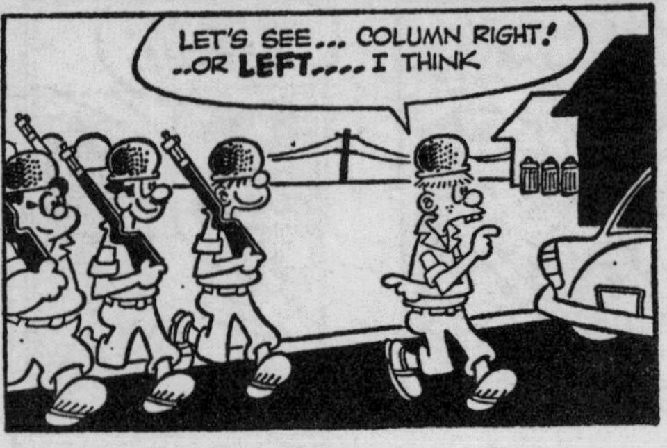
LET'S SEE... COLUMN RIGHT! ..OR LEFT..... I THINK

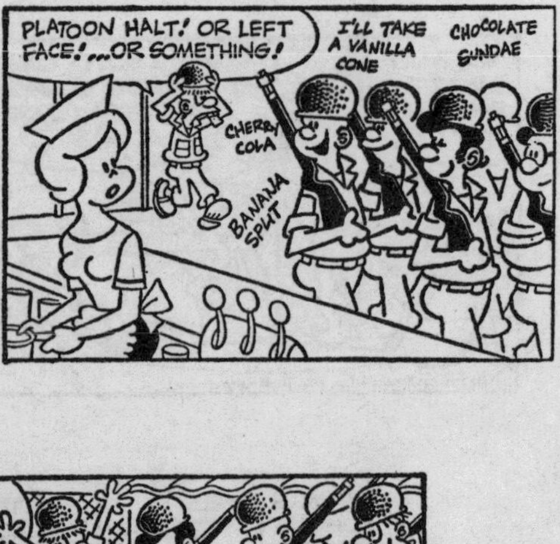
PLATOON HALT! OR LEFT FACE! ...OR SOMETHING!
I'LL TAKE A VANILLA CONE
CHOCOLATE SUNDAE
CHERRY COLA
BANANA SPLIT

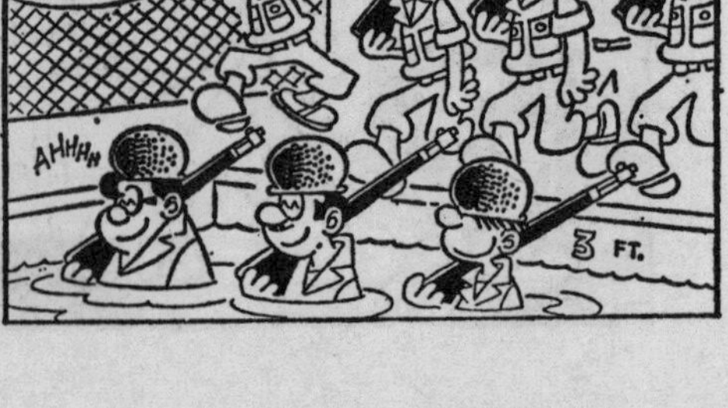
COLUMN UP! UP! I SAY!
AHHHH
3 FT.

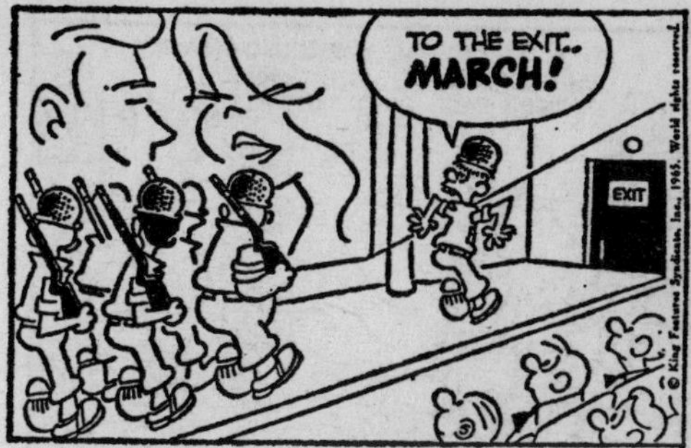
TO THE EXIT.. MARCH!
EXIT
© King Features Syndicate, Inc., 1965. World rights reserved.

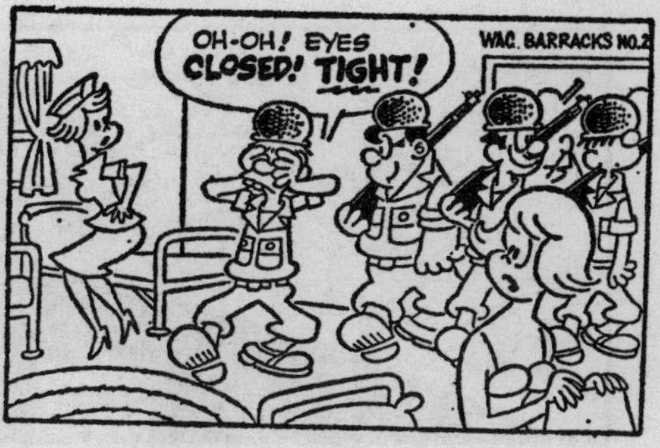
OH-OH! EYES CLOSED! TIGHT!
WAC. BARRACKS NO.2

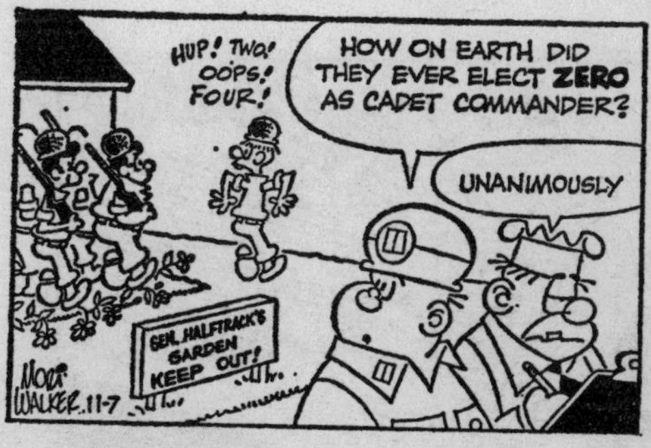
HUP! TWO! OOPS! FOUR!
HOW ON EARTH DID THEY EVER ELECT ZERO AS CADET COMMANDER?
UNANIMOUSLY
GEN. HALFTRACK'S GARDEN KEEP OUT!
MORT WALKER 11-7

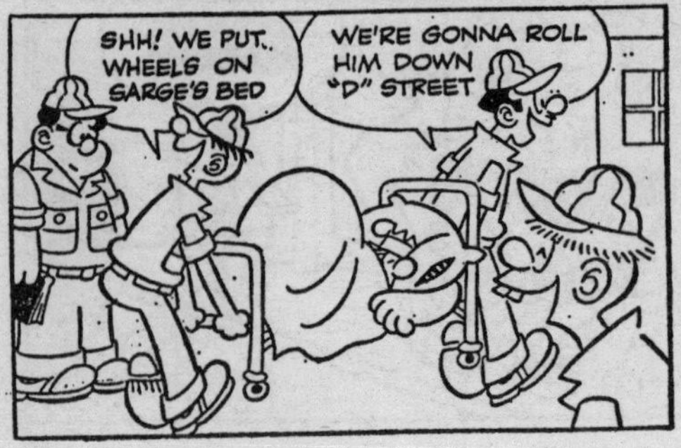
SHH! WE PUT.. WHEELS ON SARGE'S BED
WE'RE GONNA ROLL HIM DOWN "D" STREET

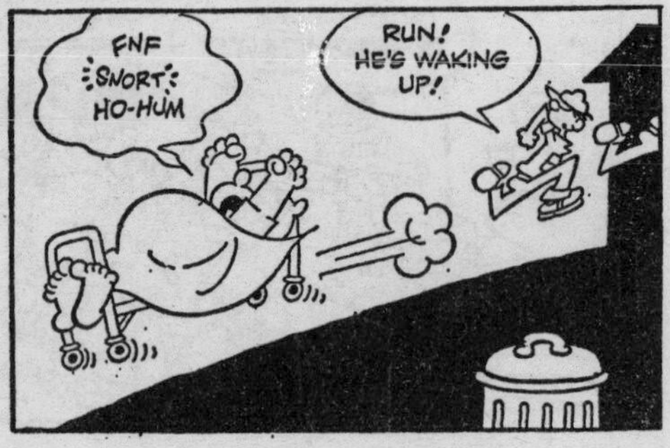
FNF SNORT HO-HUM
RUN! HE'S WAKING UP!

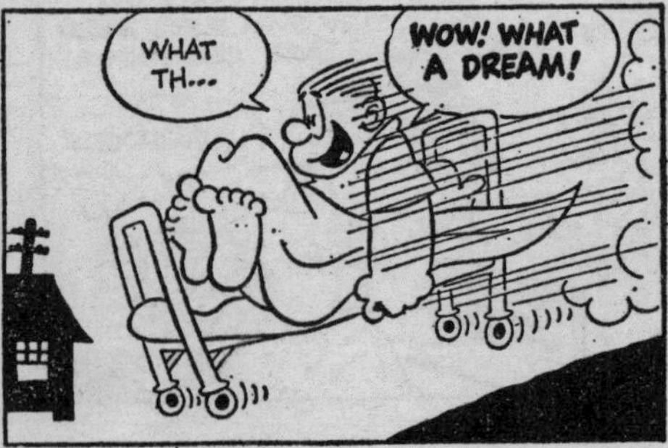
WHAT TH...
WOW! WHAT A DREAM!

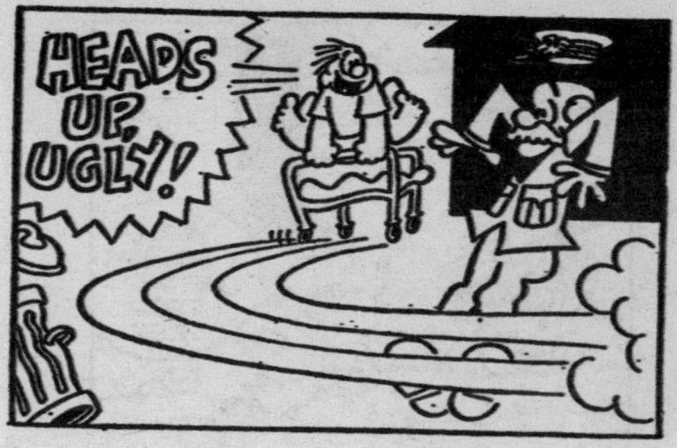
HEADS UP, UGLY!

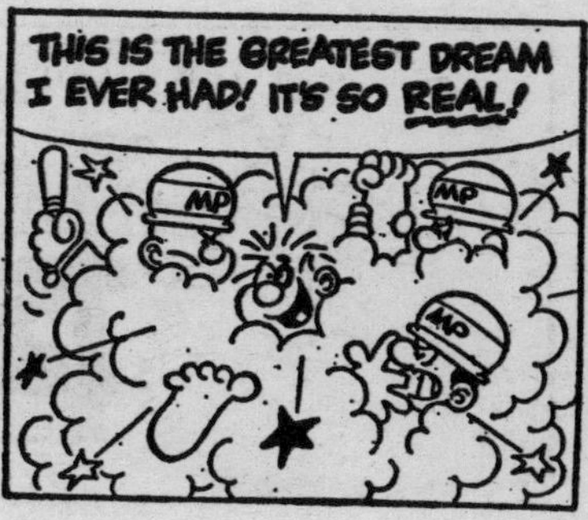
THIS IS THE GREATEST DREAM I EVER HAD! IT'S SO REAL!
MP
MP
MP

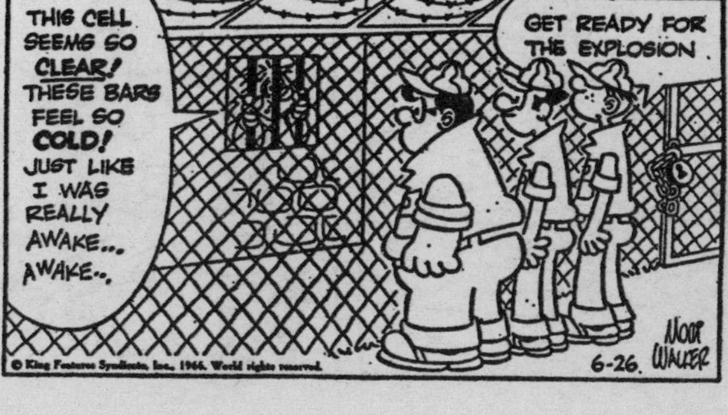
THIS CELL SEEMS SO CLEAR! THESE BARS FEEL SO COLD! JUST LIKE I WAS REALLY AWAKE... AWAKE...
GET READY FOR THE EXPLOSION
6-26.
MORT WALKER

JIGGERS, BEETLE. SARGE IS CHECKING UP ON US
YEAH, I SEE HIM BEHIND THAT TREE
HE'D REALLY LIKE TO CATCH US GOOFING OFF
HE DOESN'T REALIZE WE KNOW HE'S AROUND
I HAVE AN IDEA

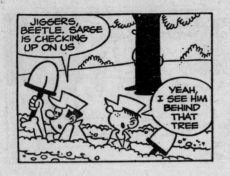

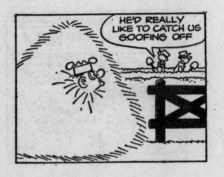

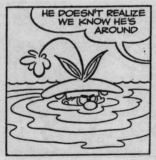

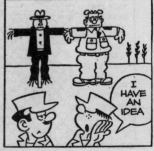

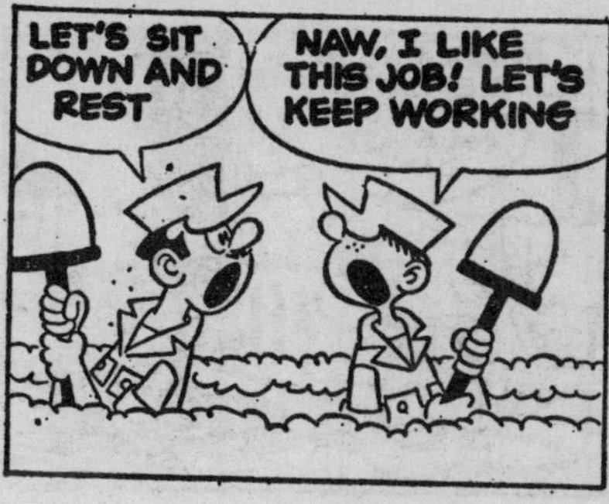
LET'S SIT DOWN AND REST
NAW, I LIKE THIS JOB! LET'S KEEP WORKING

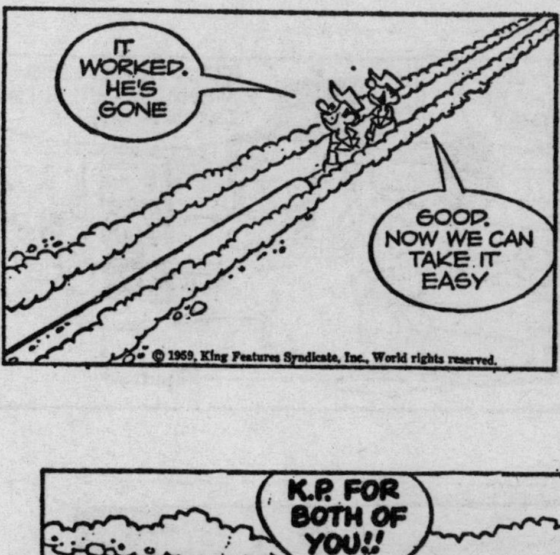
IT WORKED. HE'S GONE
GOOD. NOW WE CAN TAKE IT EASY

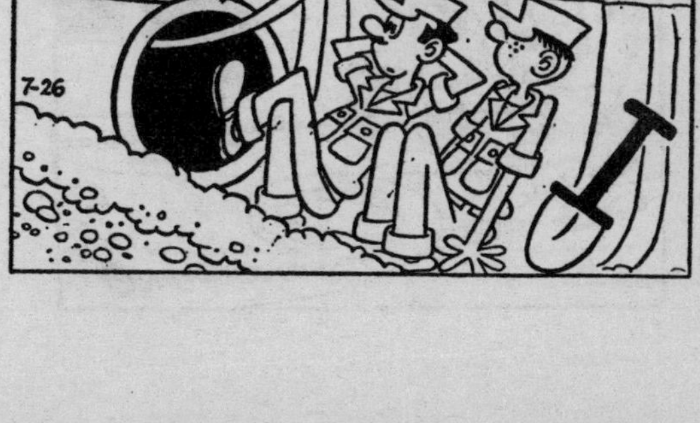
K.P. FOR BOTH OF YOU!!
7-26

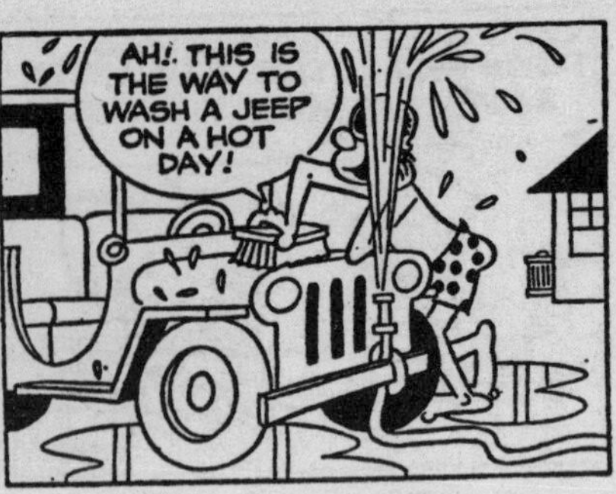
AH!. THIS IS THE WAY TO WASH A JEEP ON A HOT DAY!

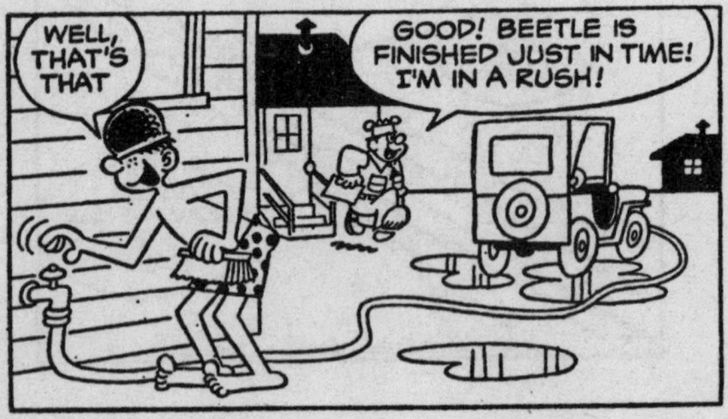
WELL, THAT'S THAT
GOOD! BEETLE IS FINISHED JUST IN TIME! I'M IN A RUSH!

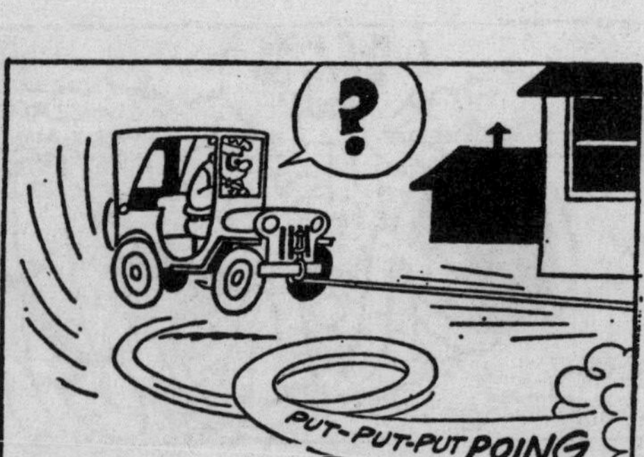
?
PUT-PUT-PUT POING

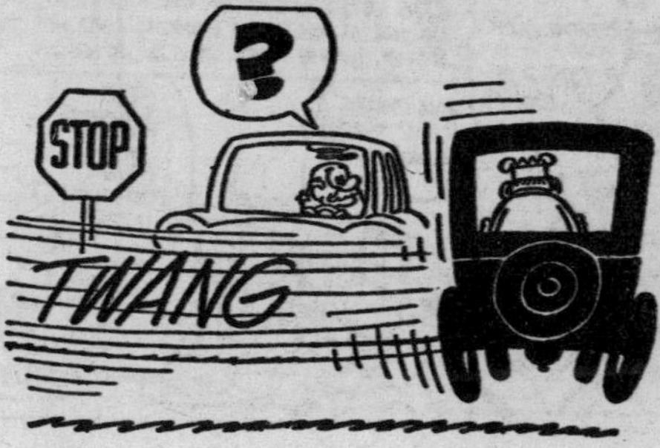
?
STOP
TWANG

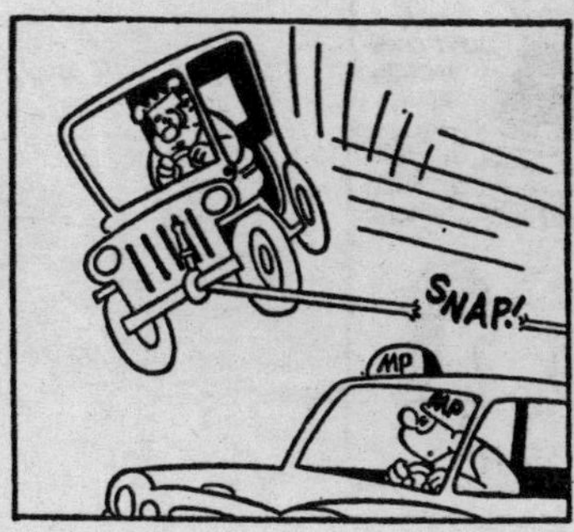
SNAP!
MP

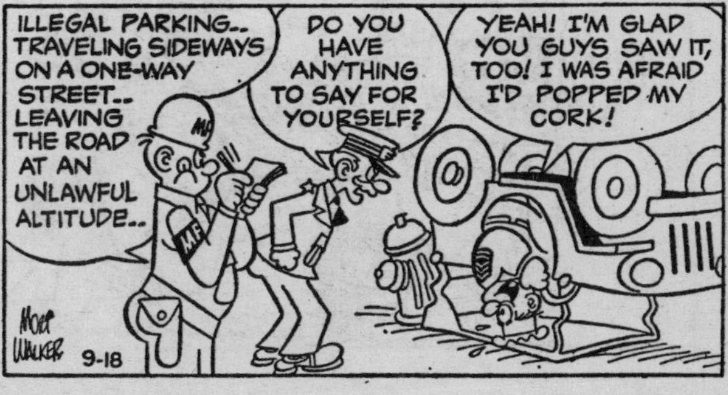
ILLEGAL PARKING.. TRAVELING SIDEWAYS ON A ONE-WAY STREET.. LEAVING THE ROAD AT AN UNLAWFUL ALTITUDE..
DO YOU HAVE ANYTHING TO SAY FOR YOURSELF?
YEAH! I'M GLAD YOU GUYS SAW IT, TOO! I WAS AFRAID I'D POPPED MY CORK!
MORT WALKER
9-18

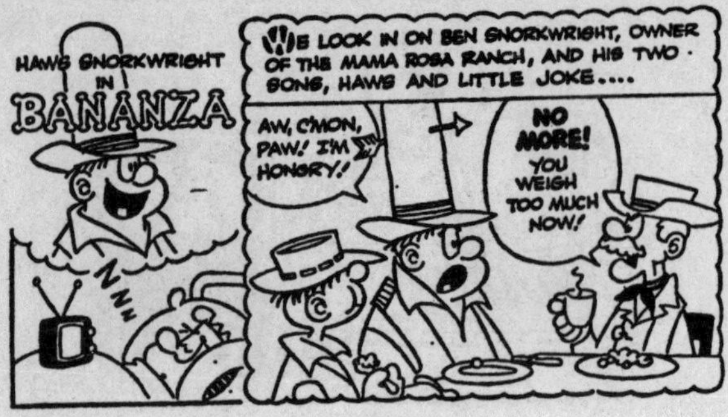
HAWS SNORKWRIGHT
IN
BANANZA
WE LOOK IN ON BEN SNORKWRIGHT, OWNER OF THE MAMA ROSA RANCH, AND HIS TWO SONS, HAWS AND LITTLE JOKE....
AW, C'MON, PAW! I'M HONGRY!
NO MORE! YOU WEIGH TOO MUCH NOW!

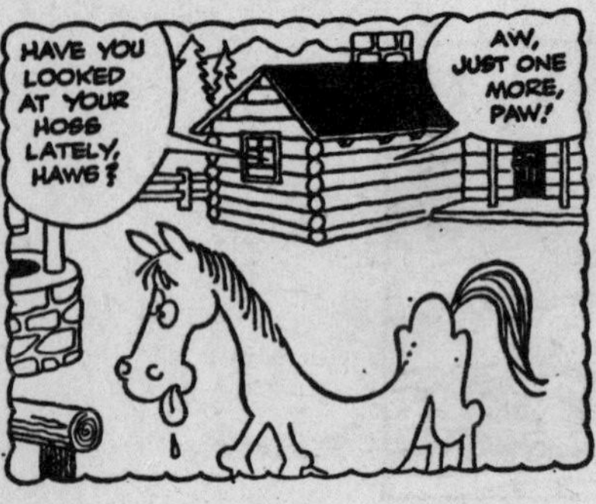
HAVE YOU LOOKED AT YOUR HOSS LATELY, HAWS?
AW, JUST ONE MORE, PAW!

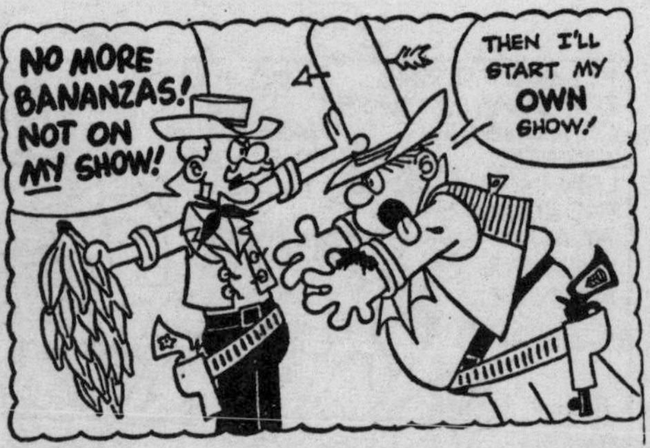
NO MORE BANANZAS! NOT ON MY SHOW!
THEN I'LL START MY OWN SHOW!

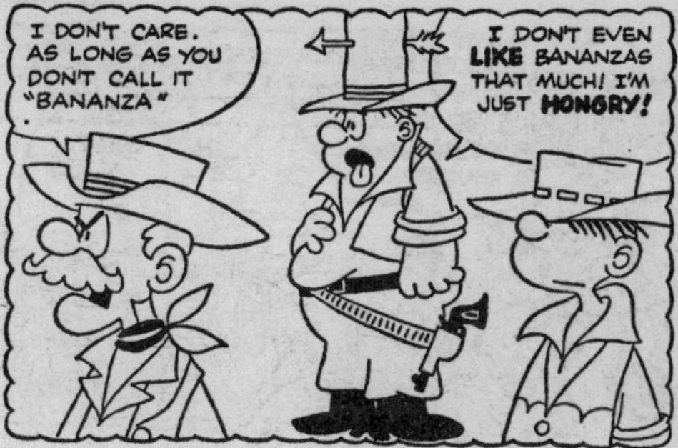
I DON'T CARE. AS LONG AS YOU DON'T CALL IT "BANANZA"
I DON'T EVEN **LIKE** BANANZAS THAT MUCH! I'M JUST **HONGRY!**

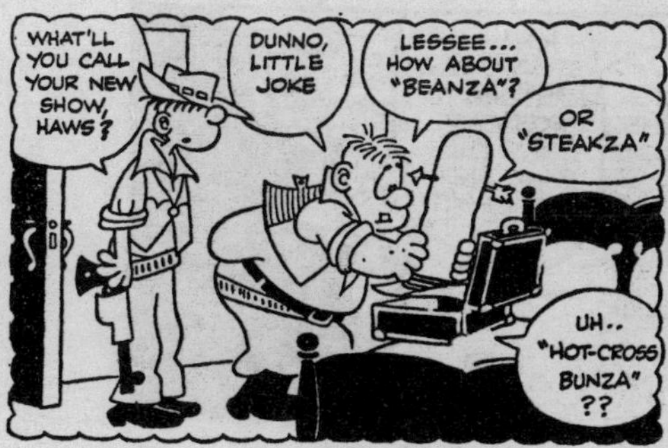
WHAT'LL YOU CALL YOUR NEW SHOW, HAWS?
DUNNO, LITTLE JOKE
LESSEE... HOW ABOUT "BEANZA"?
OR "STEAKZA"
UH.. "HOT-CROSS BUNZA" ??

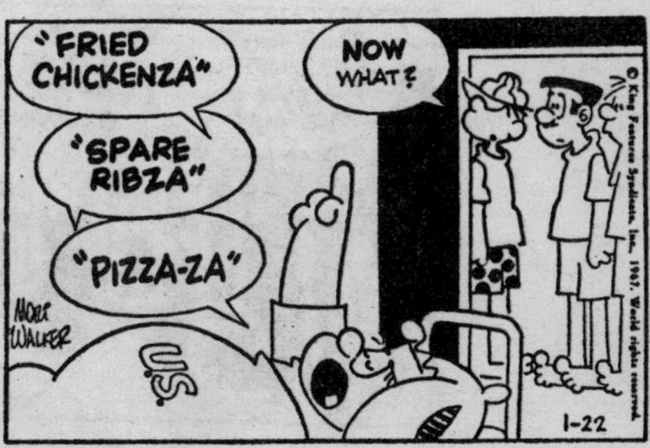
"FRIED CHICKENZA"
"SPARE RIBZA"
"PIZZA-ZA"
NOW WHAT?
MORT WALKER
U.S.
1-22
© King Features Syndicate, Inc. 1967. World rights reserved.

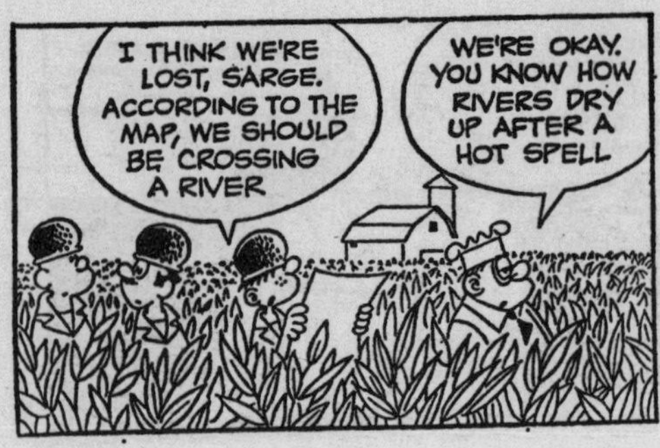
I THINK WE'RE LOST, SARGE. ACCORDING TO THE MAP, WE SHOULD BE CROSSING A RIVER
WE'RE OKAY. YOU KNOW HOW RIVERS DRY UP AFTER A HOT SPELL

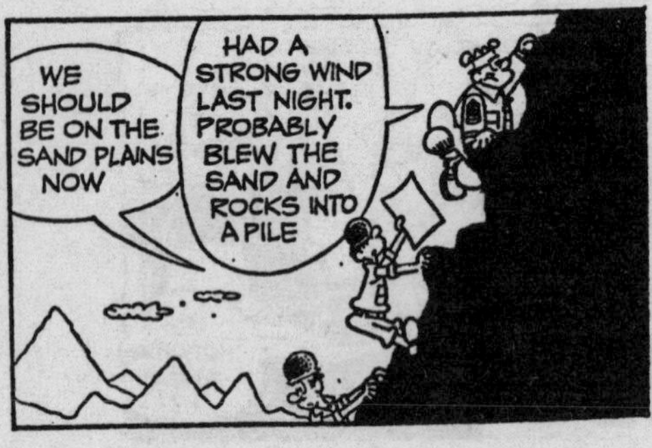
WE SHOULD BE ON THE SAND PLAINS NOW
HAD A STRONG WIND LAST NIGHT. PROBABLY BLEW THE SAND AND ROCKS INTO A PILE

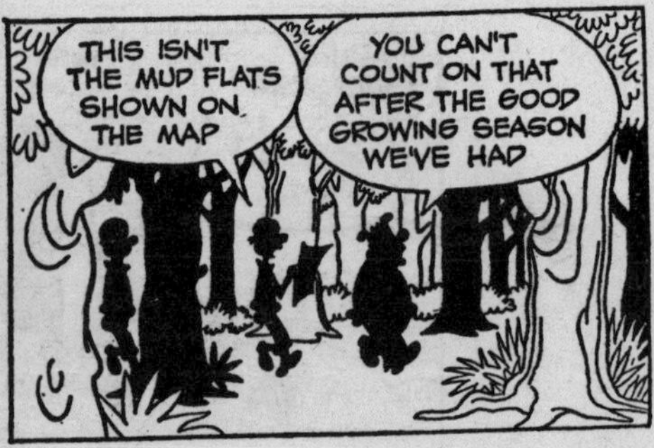
THIS ISN'T THE MUD FLATS SHOWN ON THE MAP
YOU CAN'T COUNT ON THAT AFTER THE GOOD GROWING SEASON WE'VE HAD

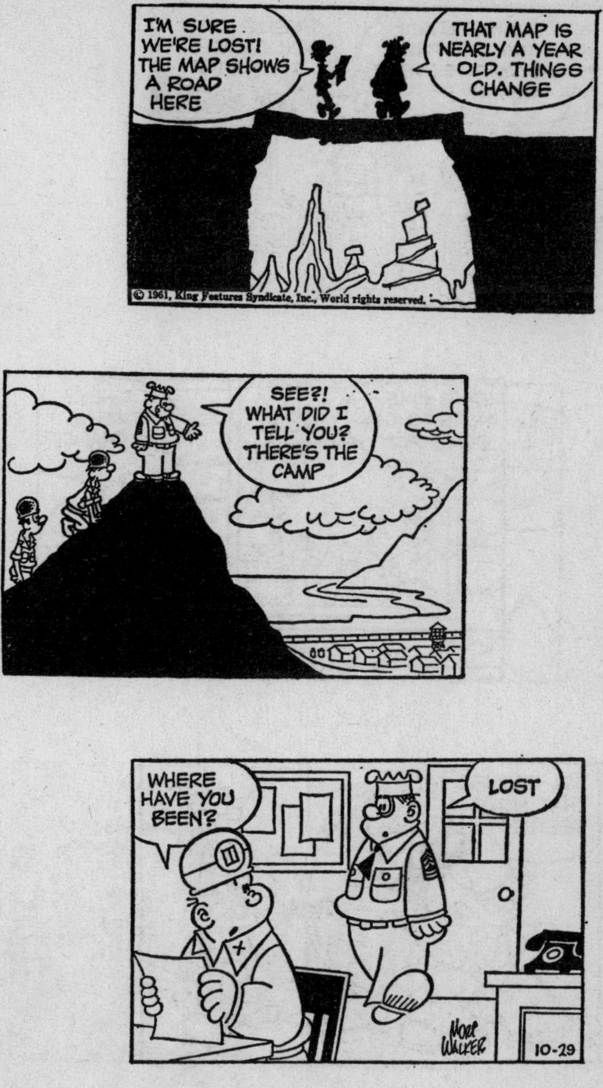
I'M SURE WE'RE LOST! THE MAP SHOWS A ROAD HERE
THAT MAP IS NEARLY A YEAR OLD. THINGS CHANGE
© 1961, King Features Syndicate, Inc., World rights reserved.
SEE?! WHAT DID I TELL YOU? THERE'S THE CAMP
WHERE HAVE YOU BEEN?
LOST
MORT WALKER
10-29

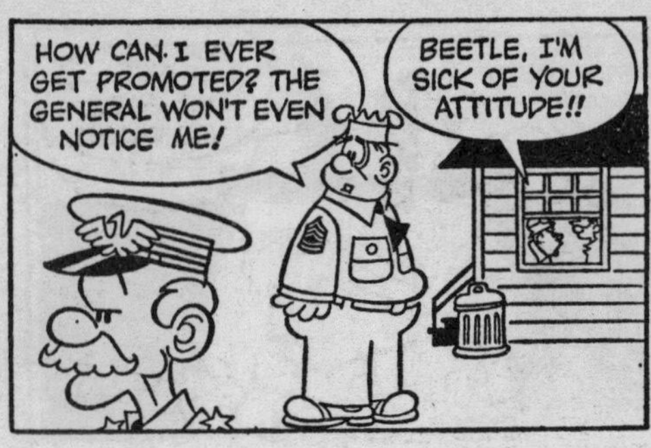
HOW CAN I EVER GET PROMOTED? THE GENERAL WON'T EVEN NOTICE ME!
BEETLE, I'M SICK OF YOUR ATTITUDE!!

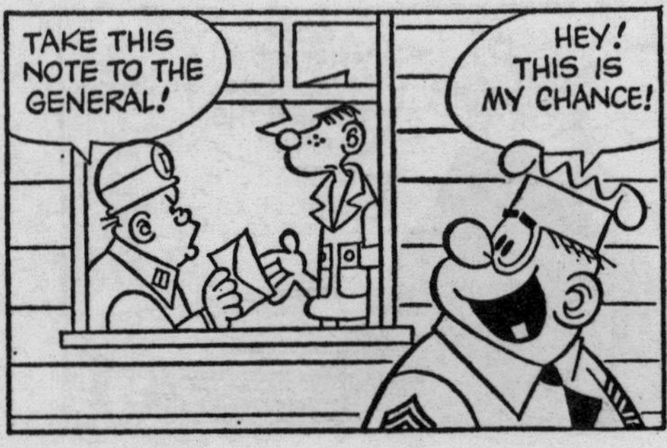
TAKE THIS NOTE TO THE GENERAL!
HEY! THIS IS MY CHANCE!

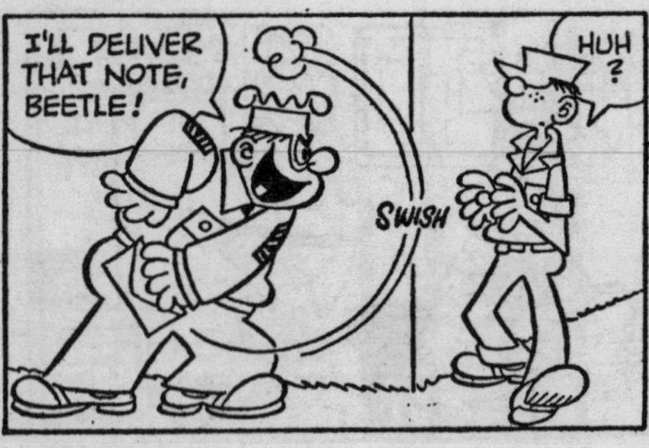
I'LL DELIVER THAT NOTE, BEETLE!
SWISH
HUH ?

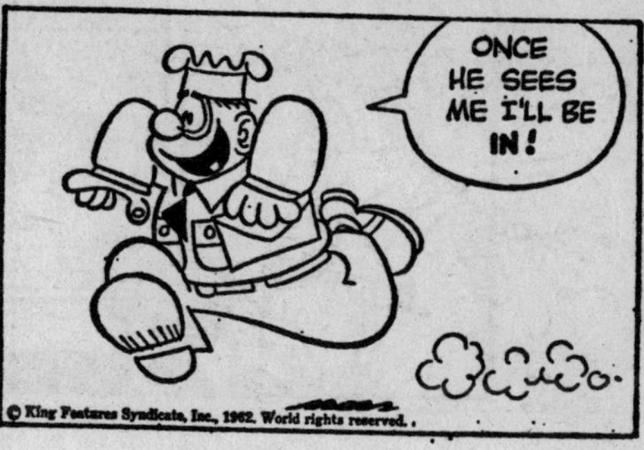
ONCE HE SEES ME I'LL BE **IN!**
© King Features Syndicate, Inc., 1962. World rights reserved.

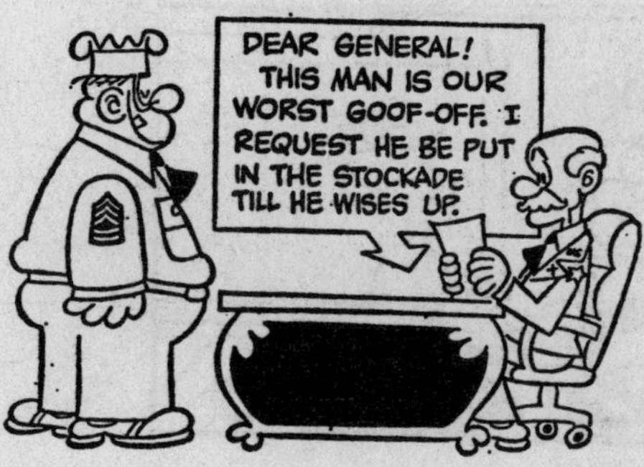
DEAR GENERAL! THIS MAN IS OUR WORST GOOF-OFF. I REQUEST HE BE PUT IN THE STOCKADE TILL HE WISES UP.

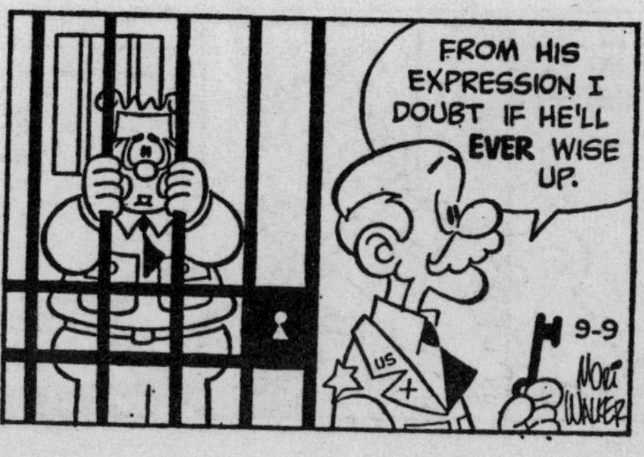
FROM HIS EXPRESSION I DOUBT IF HE'LL **EVER** WISE UP.
9-9
MORT WALKER

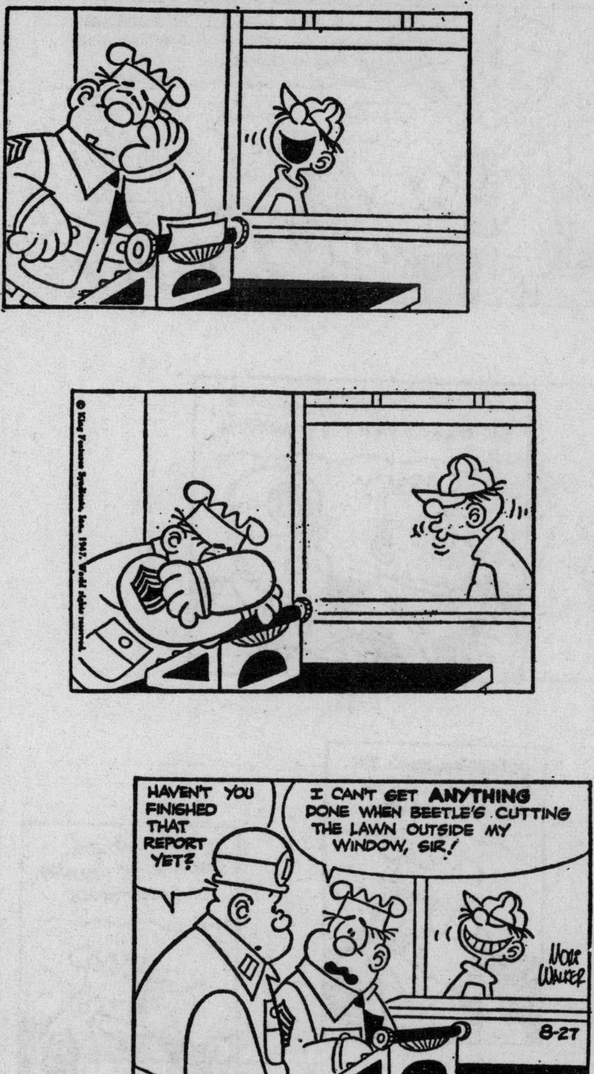
© King Features Syndicate, Inc., 1987. World rights reserved.
HAVEN'T YOU FINISHED THAT REPORT YET?
I CAN'T GET **ANYTHING** DONE WHEN BEETLE'S CUTTING THE LAWN OUTSIDE MY WINDOW, SIR!
MORT WALKER
8-27

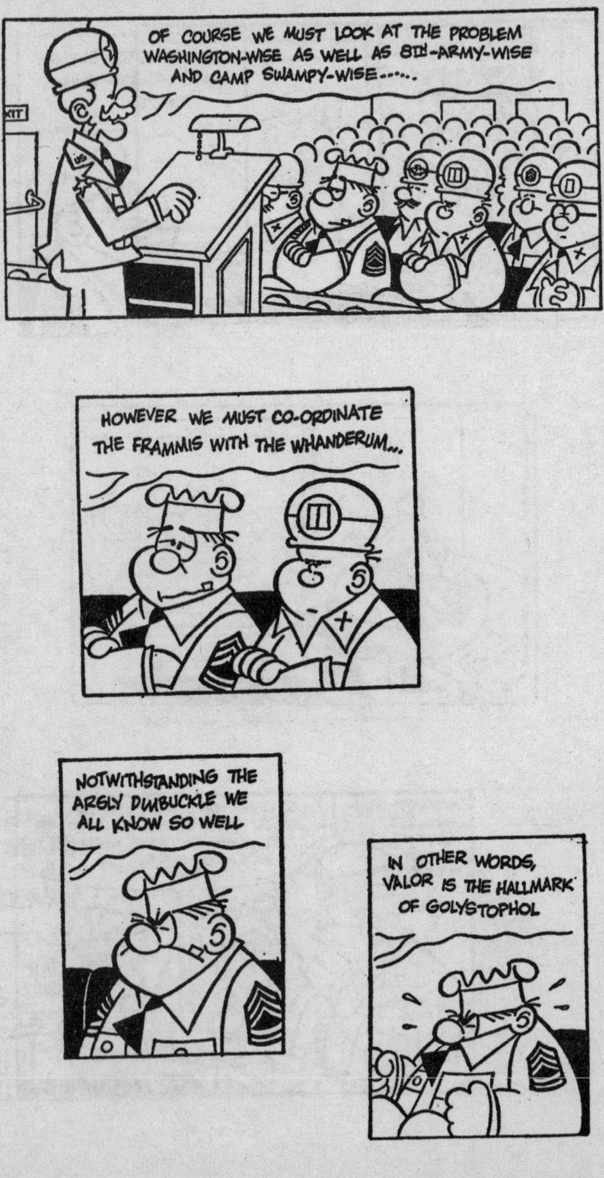
OF COURSE WE MUST LOOK AT THE PROBLEM WASHINGTON-WISE AS WELL AS 8TH-ARMY-WISE AND CAMP SWAMPY-WISE......
EXIT
HOWEVER WE MUST CO-ORDINATE THE FRAMMIS WITH THE WHANDERUM...
NOTWITHSTANDING THE ARGLY DIMBUCKLE WE ALL KNOW SO WELL
IN OTHER WORDS, VALOR IS THE HALLMARK OF GOLYSTOPHOL

AS VAN DRUSEL USED TO SAY, "WHEN ARE THEY NOT?"
AND I'VE OFTEN THOUGHT GAR GRIMFEL DUNK MYSELF
AND, ER... WELL... I GUESS THAT'S ALL I HAVE TO SAY
US
FOR GOSH SAKES! YOU SHOULDN'T SIT THERE MAKING FACES AT THE GENERAL!
I WAS STIFLING A YAWN!
MORT WALKER
4-11

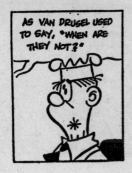

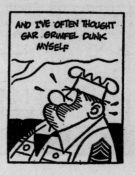

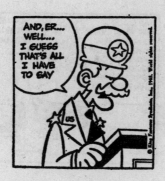

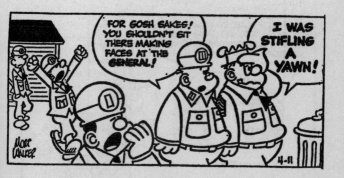

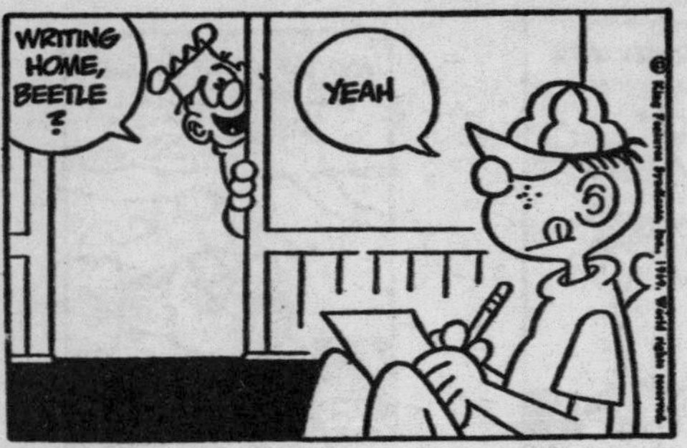
WRITING HOME, BEETLE?
YEAH

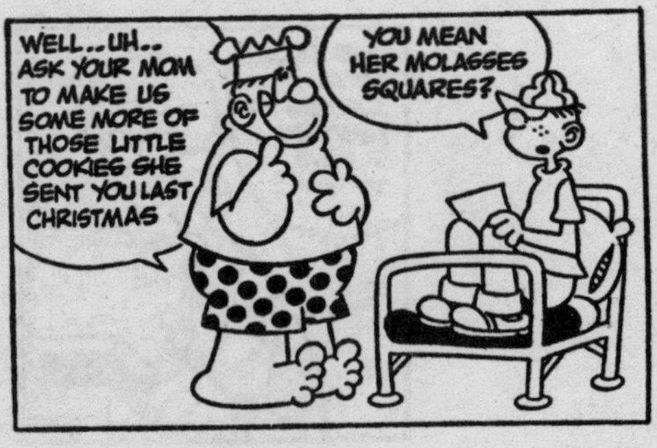
WELL..UH.. ASK YOUR MOM TO MAKE US SOME MORE OF THOSE LITTLE COOKIES SHE SENT YOU LAST CHRISTMAS
YOU MEAN HER MOLASSES SQUARES?

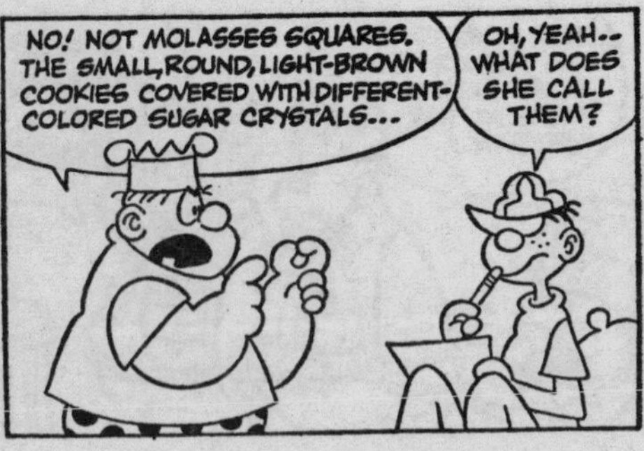
NO! NOT MOLASSES SQUARES. THE SMALL, ROUND, LIGHT-BROWN COOKIES COVERED WITH DIFFERENT-COLORED SUGAR CRYSTALS...
OH, YEAH.. WHAT DOES SHE CALL THEM?

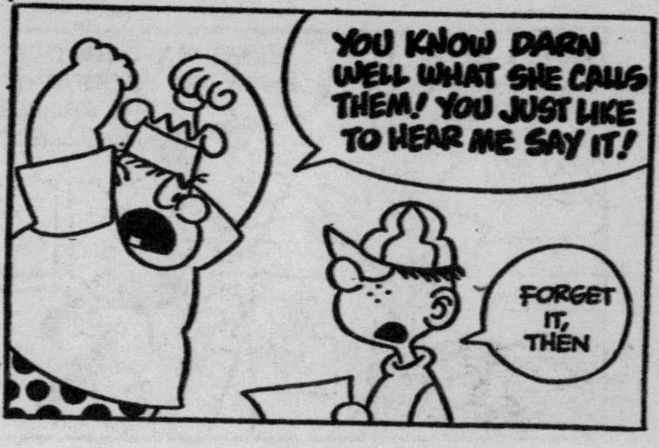
YOU KNOW DARN WELL WHAT SHE CALLS THEM! YOU JUST LIKE TO HEAR ME SAY IT!
FORGET IT, THEN

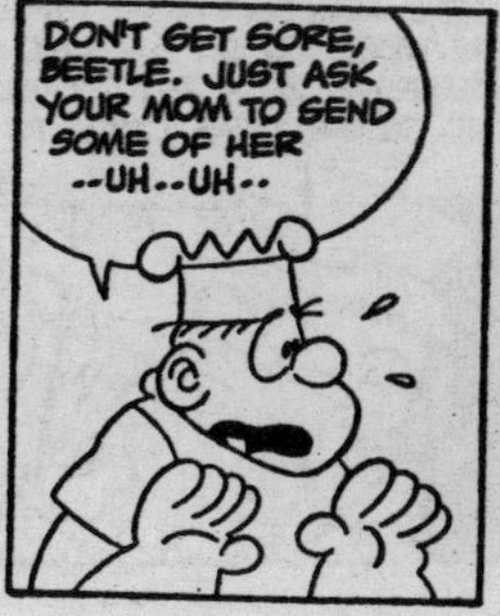
DON'T GET SORE, BEETLE. JUST ASK YOUR MOM TO SEND SOME OF HER --UH--UH--

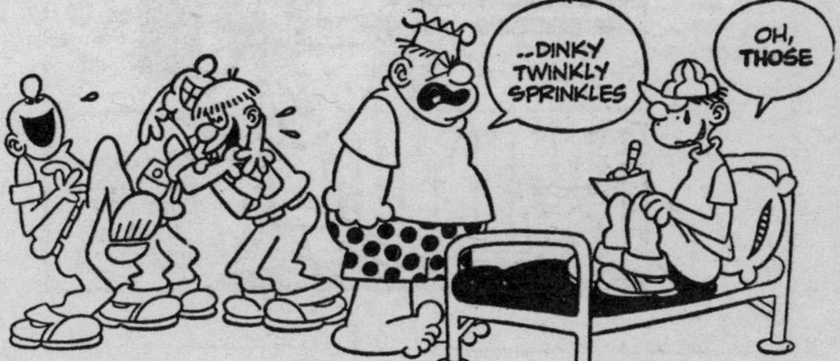
--DINKY TWINKLY SPRINKLES
OH, THOSE

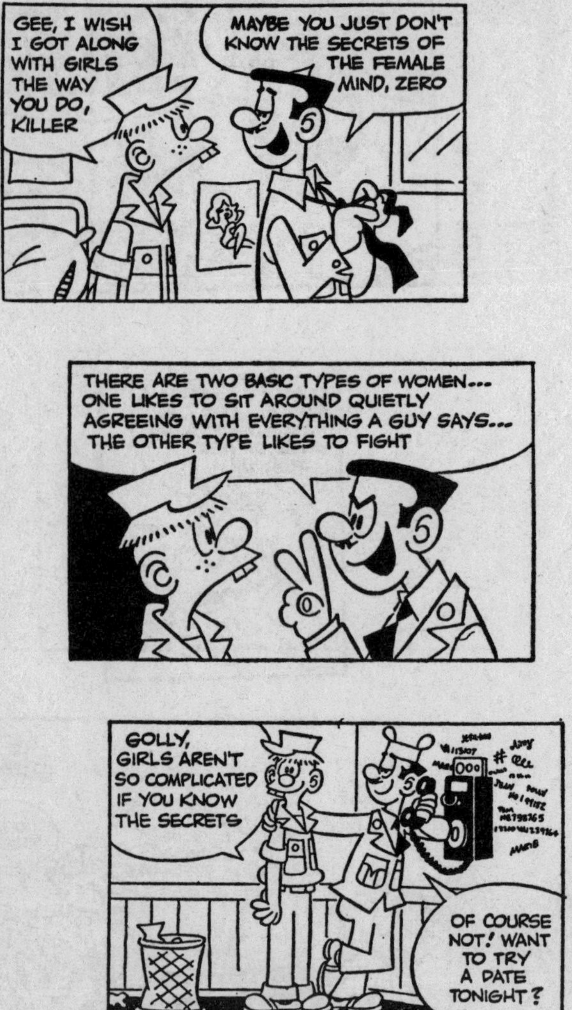
GEE, I WISH I GOT ALONG WITH GIRLS THE WAY YOU DO, KILLER
MAYBE YOU JUST DON'T KNOW THE SECRETS OF THE FEMALE MIND, ZERO
THERE ARE TWO BASIC TYPES OF WOMEN... ONE LIKES TO SIT AROUND QUIETLY AGREEING WITH EVERYTHING A GUY SAYS... THE OTHER TYPE LIKES TO FIGHT
GOLLY, GIRLS AREN'T SO COMPLICATED IF YOU KNOW THE SECRETS
OF COURSE NOT! WANT TO TRY A DATE TONIGHT?

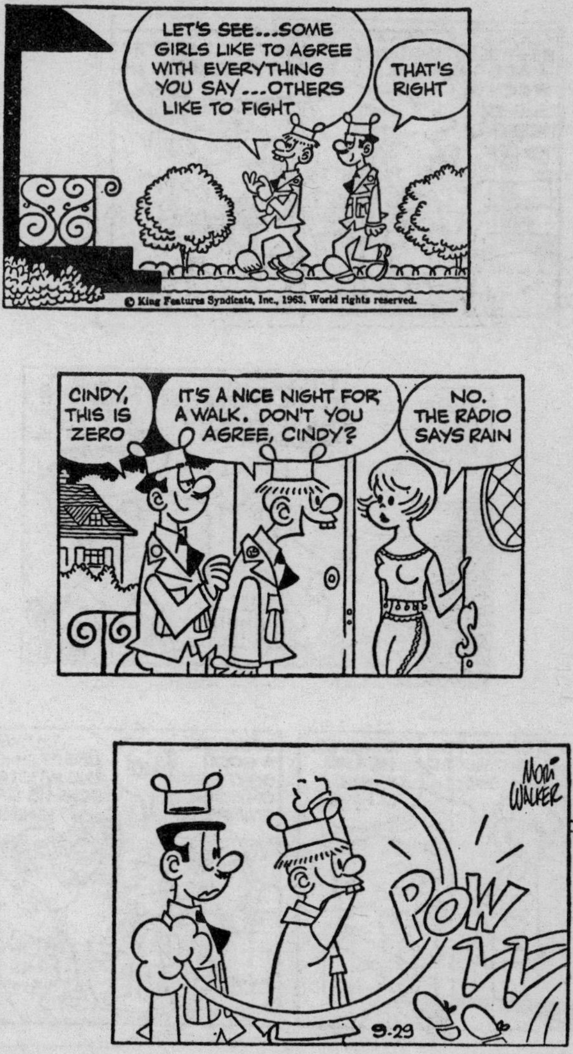
LET'S SEE...SOME GIRLS LIKE TO AGREE WITH EVERYTHING YOU SAY...OTHERS LIKE TO FIGHT
THAT'S RIGHT
CINDY, THIS IS ZERO
IT'S A NICE NIGHT FOR A WALK. DON'T YOU AGREE, CINDY?
NO. THE RADIO SAYS RAIN
MORT WALKER
POW
9-29

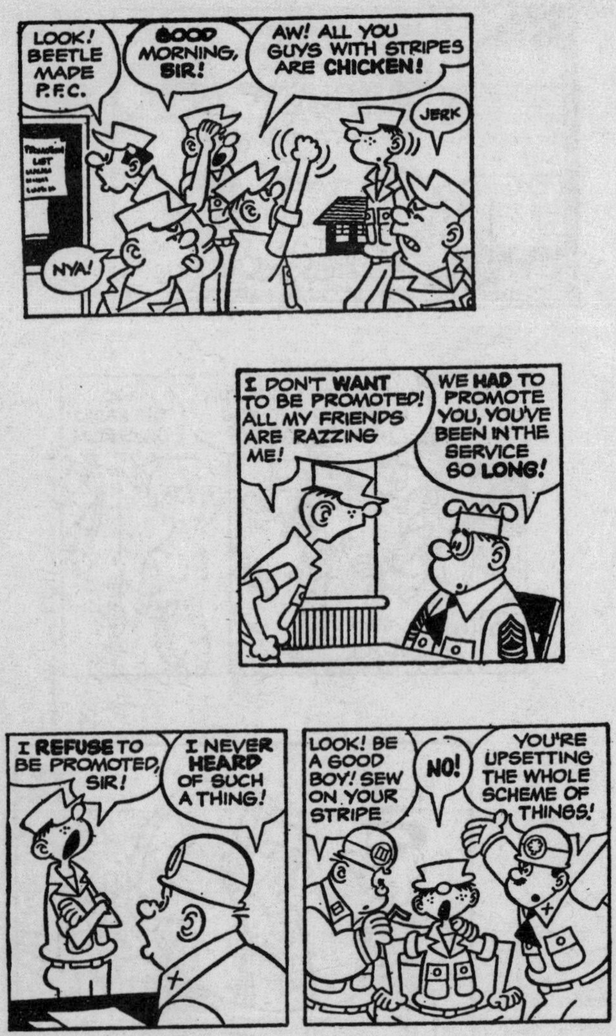
LOOK! BEETLE MADE P.F.C.
GOOD MORNING, SIR!
AW! ALL YOU GUYS WITH STRIPES ARE CHICKEN!
JERK
NYA!
I DON'T WANT TO BE PROMOTED! ALL MY FRIENDS ARE RAZZING ME!
WE HAD TO PROMOTE YOU, YOU'VE BEEN IN THE SERVICE SO LONG!
I REFUSE TO BE PROMOTED, SIR!
I NEVER HEARD OF SUCH A THING!
LOOK! BE A GOOD BOY! SEW ON YOUR STRIPE
NO!
YOU'RE UPSETTING THE WHOLE SCHEME OF THINGS!

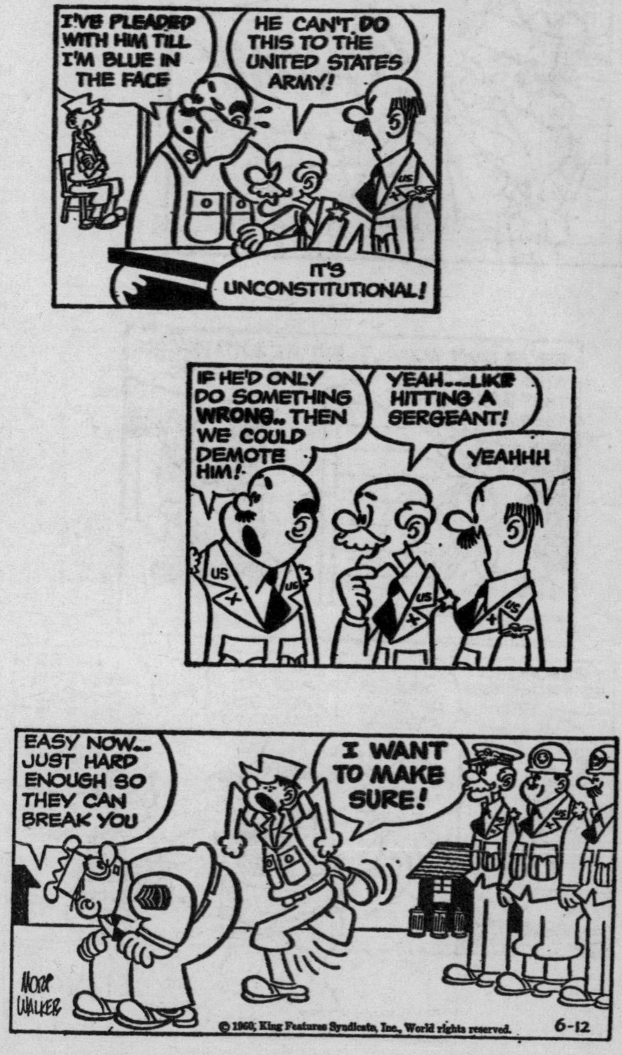
I'VE PLEADED WITH HIM TILL I'M BLUE IN THE FACE
HE CAN'T DO THIS TO THE UNITED STATES ARMY!
IT'S UNCONSTITUTIONAL!
IF HE'D ONLY DO SOMETHING WRONG.. THEN WE COULD DEMOTE HIM!
YEAH...LIKE HITTING A SERGEANT!
YEAHHH
EASY NOW... JUST HARD ENOUGH SO THEY CAN BREAK YOU
I WANT TO MAKE SURE!
MORT WALKER
© 1960, King Features Syndicate, Inc., World rights reserved.
6-12

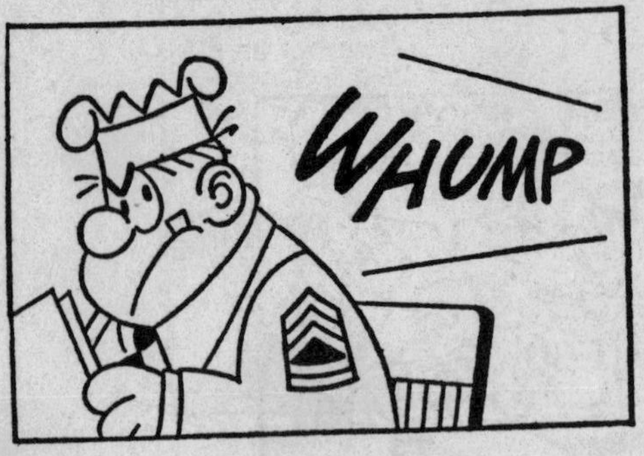
WHUMP

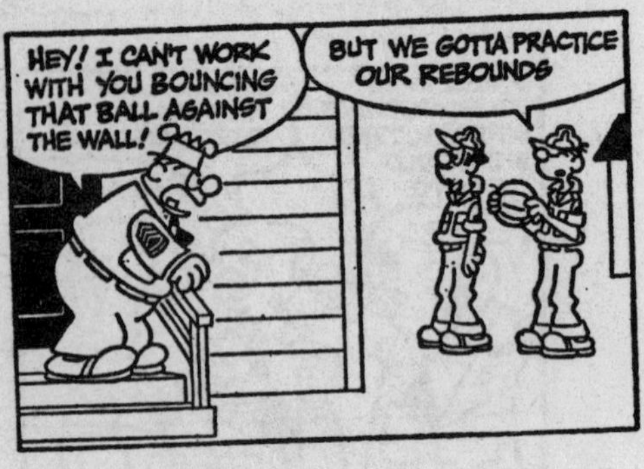
HEY! I CAN'T WORK WITH YOU BOUNCING THAT BALL AGAINST THE WALL!
BUT WE GOTTA PRACTICE OUR REBOUNDS

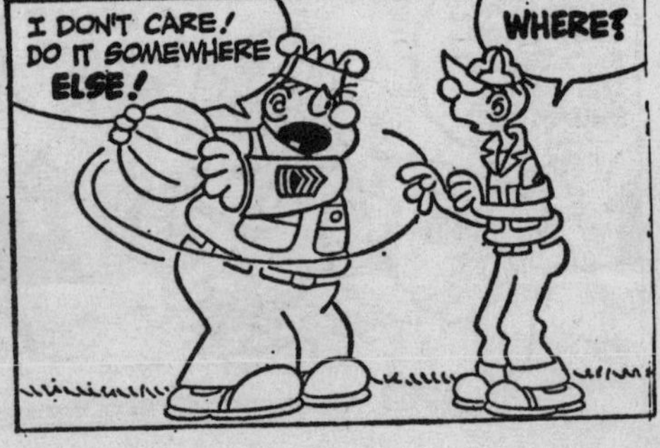
I DON'T CARE! DO IT SOMEWHERE ELSE!
WHERE?

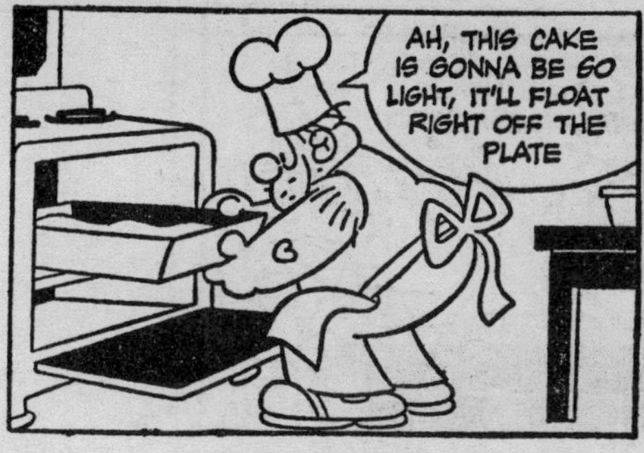
AH, THIS CAKE IS GONNA BE SO LIGHT, IT'LL FLOAT RIGHT OFF THE PLATE

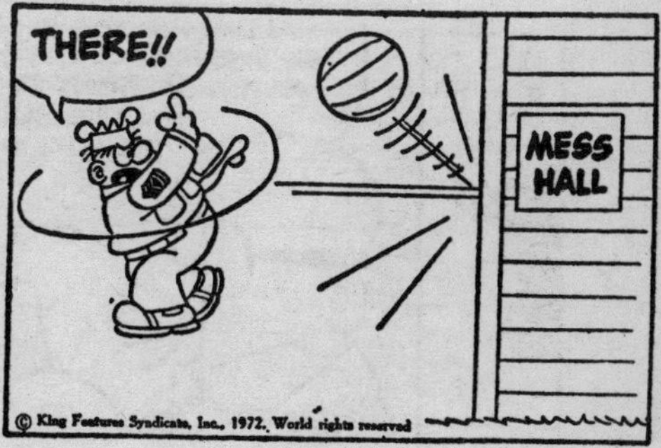
THERE!!
MESS HALL
© King Features Syndicate, Inc., 1972. World rights reserved

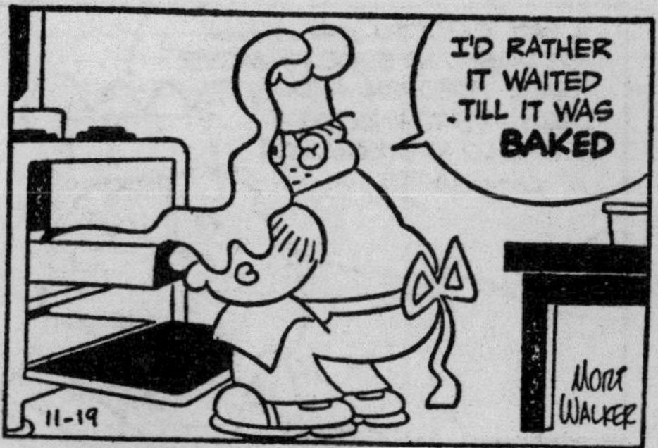
I'D RATHER IT WAITED TILL IT WAS BAKED
11-19
MORT WALKER

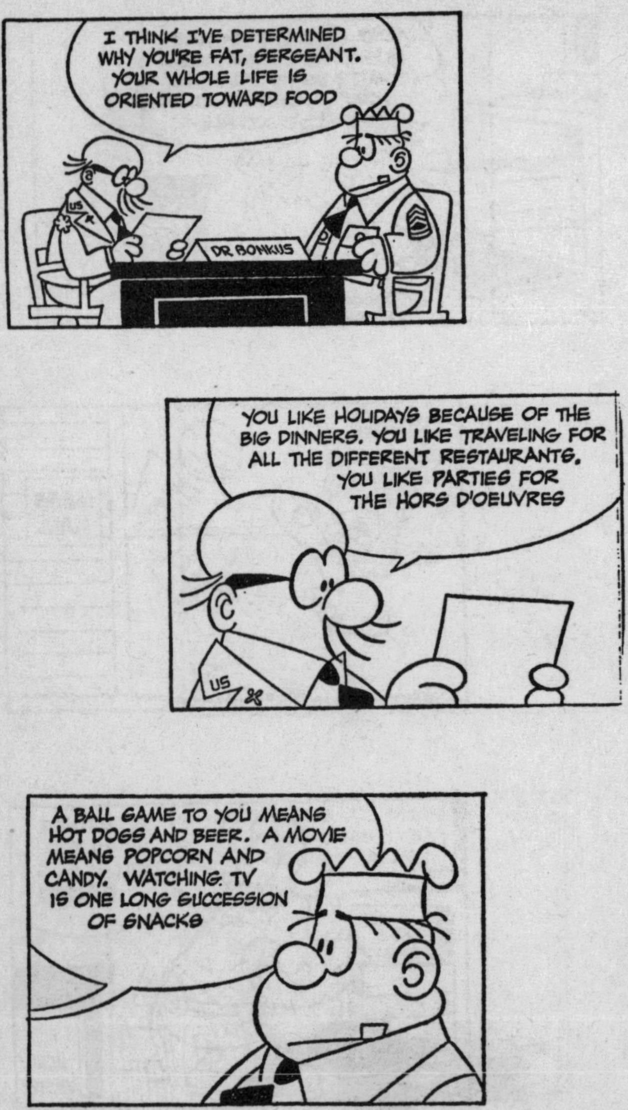
I THINK I'VE DETERMINED WHY YOU'RE FAT, SERGEANT. YOUR WHOLE LIFE IS ORIENTED TOWARD FOOD
DR BONKUS
YOU LIKE HOLIDAYS BECAUSE OF THE BIG DINNERS. YOU LIKE TRAVELING FOR ALL THE DIFFERENT RESTAURANTS. YOU LIKE PARTIES FOR THE HORS D'OEUVRES
A BALL GAME TO YOU MEANS HOT DOGS AND BEER. A MOVIE MEANS POPCORN AND CANDY. WATCHING TV IS ONE LONG SUCCESSION OF SNACKS

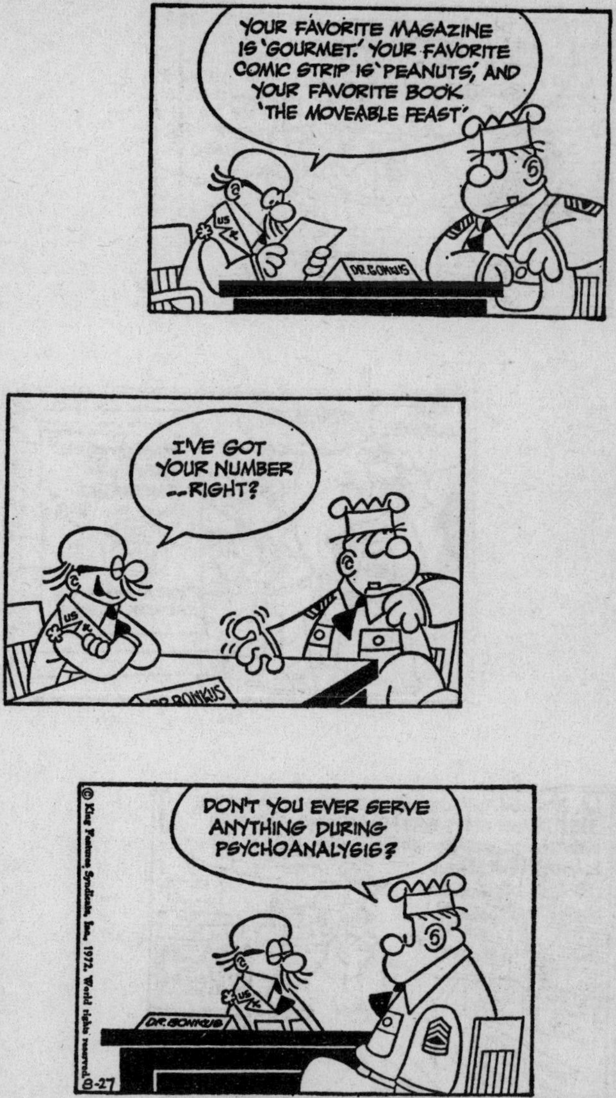
YOUR FAVORITE MAGAZINE IS 'GOURMET.' YOUR FAVORITE COMIC STRIP IS 'PEANUTS,' AND YOUR FAVORITE BOOK 'THE MOVEABLE FEAST.'
DR. BONKUS
I'VE GOT YOUR NUMBER --RIGHT?
DON'T YOU EVER SERVE ANYTHING DURING PSYCHOANALYSIS?
DR. BONKUS
© King Features Syndicate, Inc., 1972. World rights reserved.
8-27

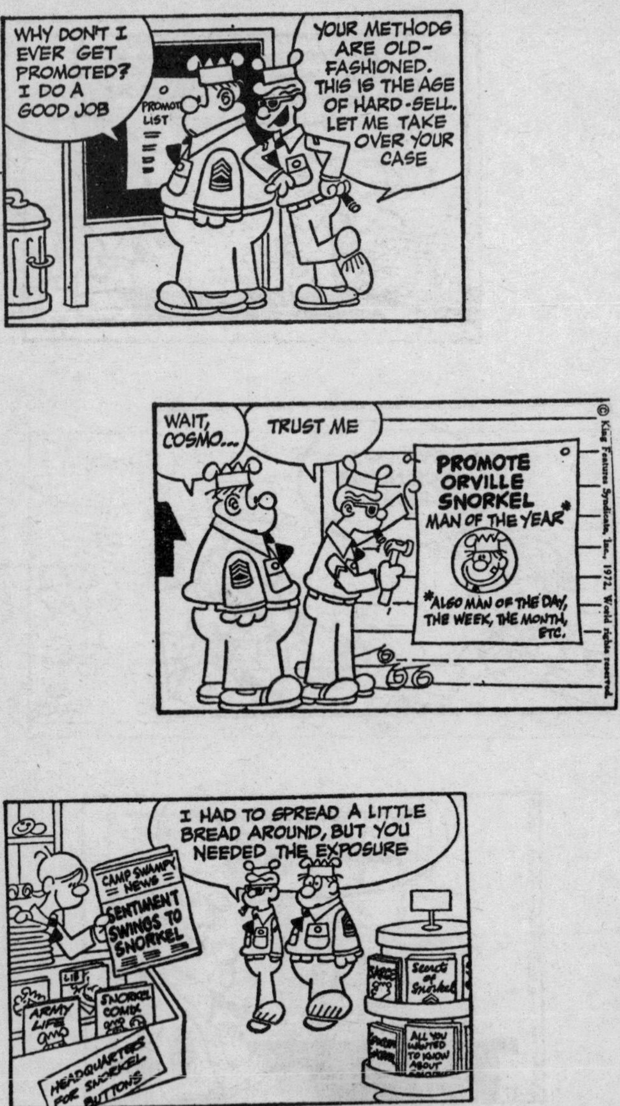
WHY DON'T I EVER GET PROMOTED? I DO A GOOD JOB
PROMOT LIST
YOUR METHODS ARE OLD-FASHIONED. THIS IS THE AGE OF HARD-SELL. LET ME TAKE OVER YOUR CASE
WAIT, COSMO...
TRUST ME
PROMOTE ORVILLE SNORKEL MAN OF THE YEAR*
*ALSO MAN OF THE DAY, THE WEEK, THE MONTH, ETC.
© King Features Syndicate, Inc., 1972. World rights reserved.
I HAD TO SPREAD A LITTLE BREAD AROUND, BUT YOU NEEDED THE EXPOSURE
CAMP SWAMPY NEWS
SENTIMENT SWINGS TO SNORKEL
ARMY LIFE
SNORKEL COMIX
HEADQUARTERS FOR SNORKEL BUTTONS
Secrets of Snorkel
ALL YOU WANTED TO KNOW ABOUT

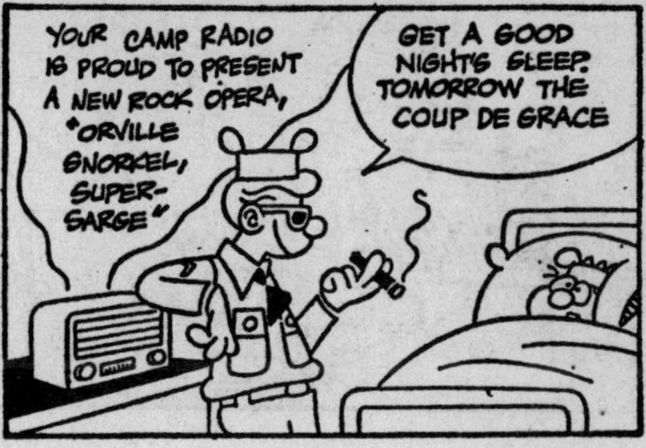
YOUR CAMP RADIO IS PROUD TO PRESENT A NEW ROCK OPERA, "ORVILLE SNORKEL, SUPER-SARGE"
GET A GOOD NIGHT'S SLEEP. TOMORROW THE COUP DE GRACE

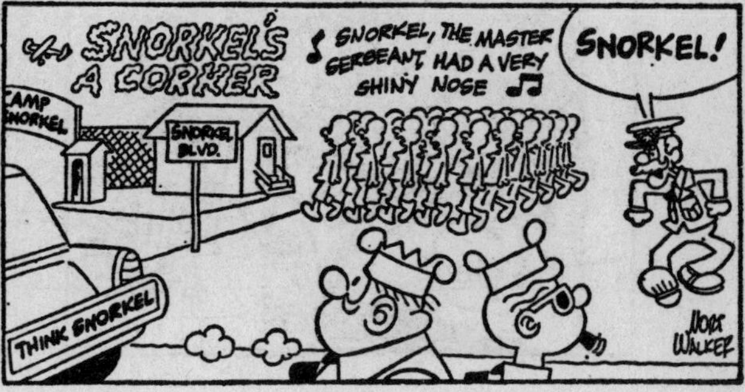
SNORKEL'S A CORKER
SNORKEL, THE MASTER SERGEANT, HAD A VERY SHINY NOSE
SNORKEL!
CAMP SNORKEL
SNORKEL BLVD.
THINK SNORKEL
MORT WALKER

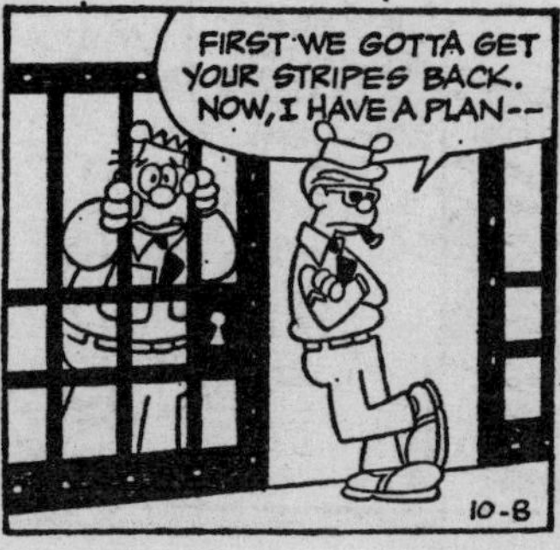
FIRST WE GOTTA GET YOUR STRIPES BACK. NOW, I HAVE A PLAN--
10-8

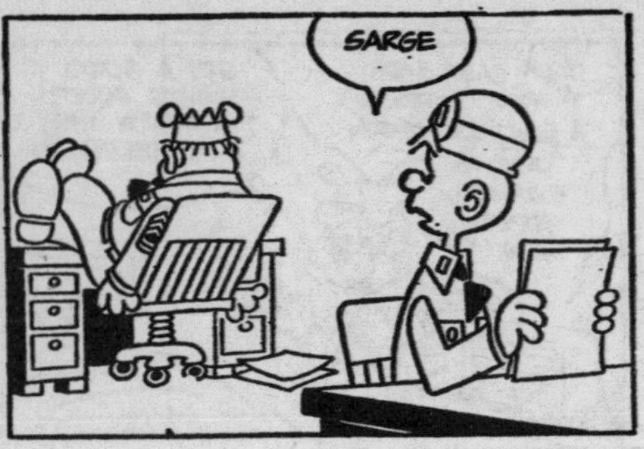
SARGE

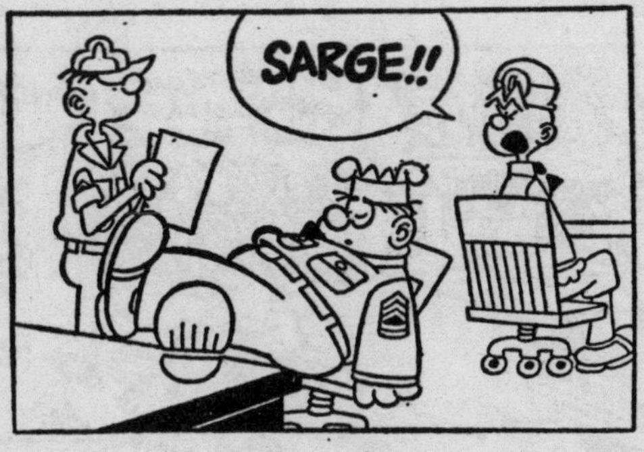
SARGE!!

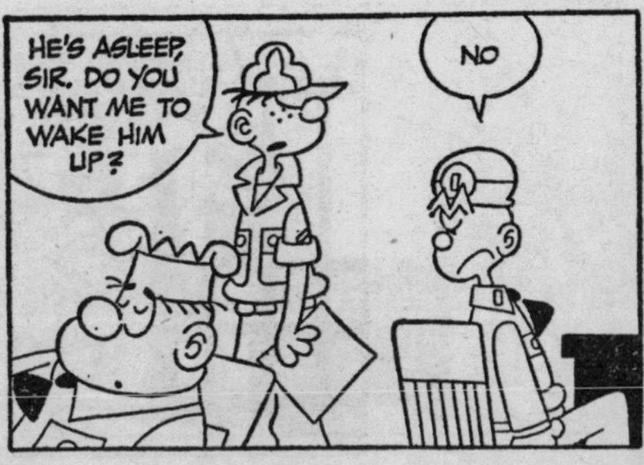
HE'S ASLEEP, SIR. DO YOU WANT ME TO WAKE HIM UP?
NO

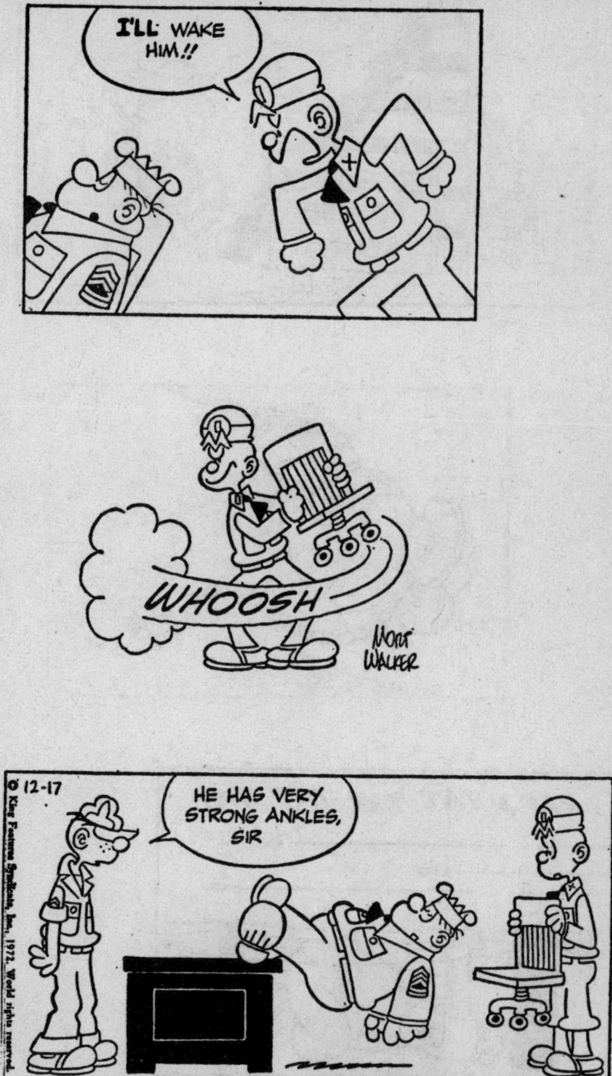
I'LL WAKE HIM!!
WHOOSH
MORT WALKER
© 12-17
King Features Syndicate, Inc., 1972. World rights reserved.
HE HAS VERY STRONG ANKLES, SIR

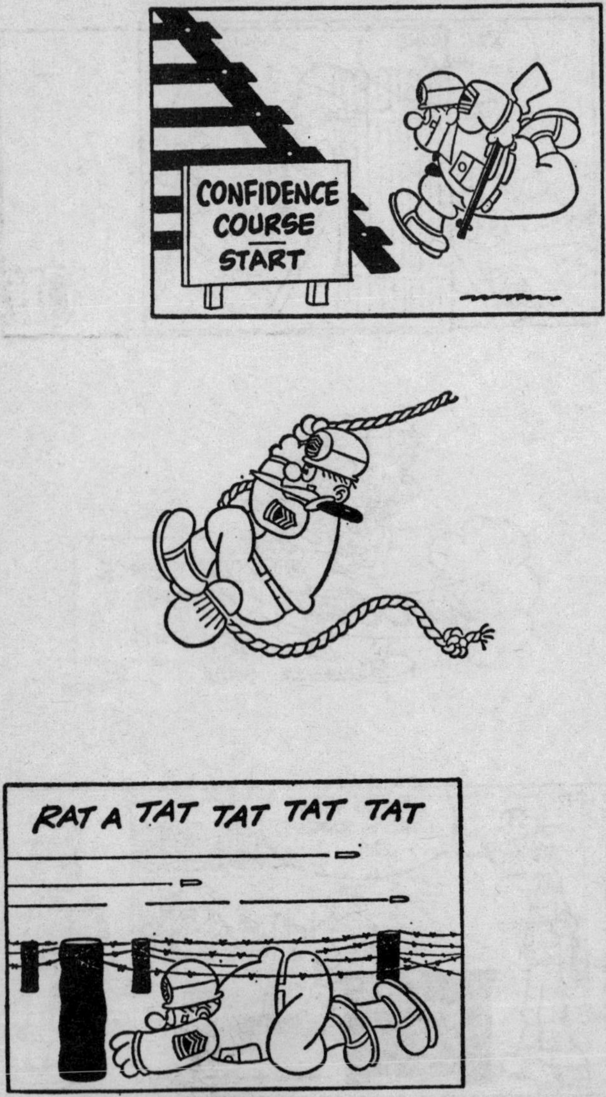
CONFIDENCE
COURSE
START
RAT A TAT TAT TAT TAT

CONFIDENCE
COURSE
FINISH
3-19

I DUNNO...I STILL DON'T FEEL CONFIDENT
SERVICE CLUB
MORT WALKER

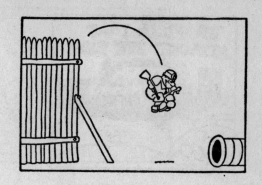

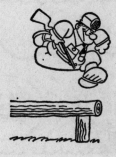

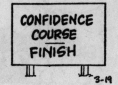

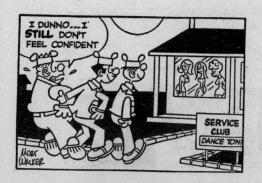

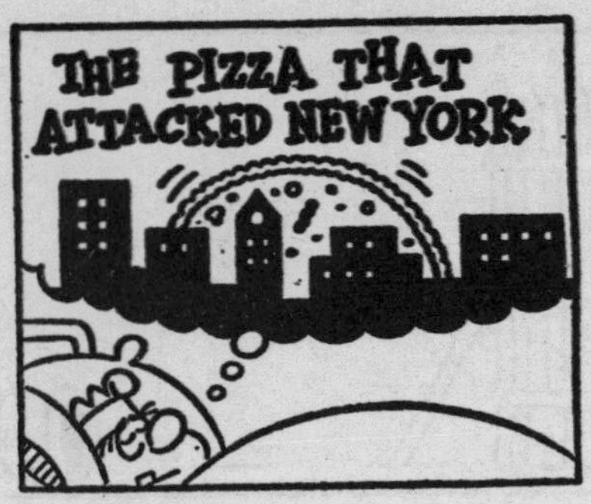
THE PIZZA THAT ATTACKED NEW YORK

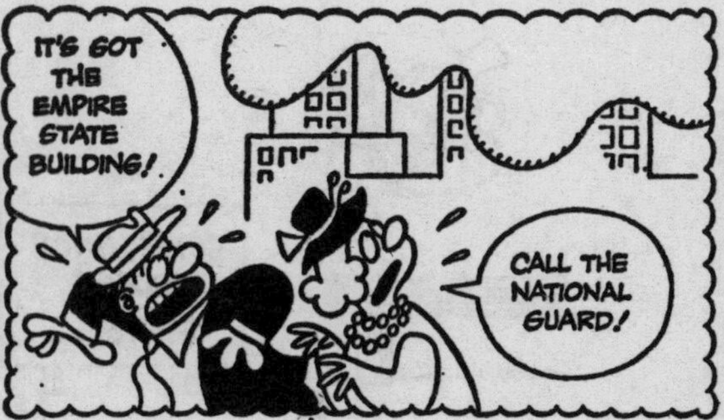
IT'S GOT THE EMPIRE STATE BUILDING!
CALL THE NATIONAL GUARD!

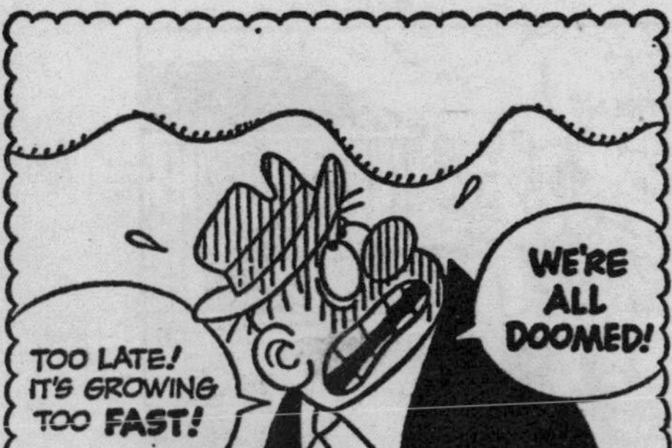
TOO LATE! IT'S GROWING TOO FAST!
WE'RE ALL DOOMED!

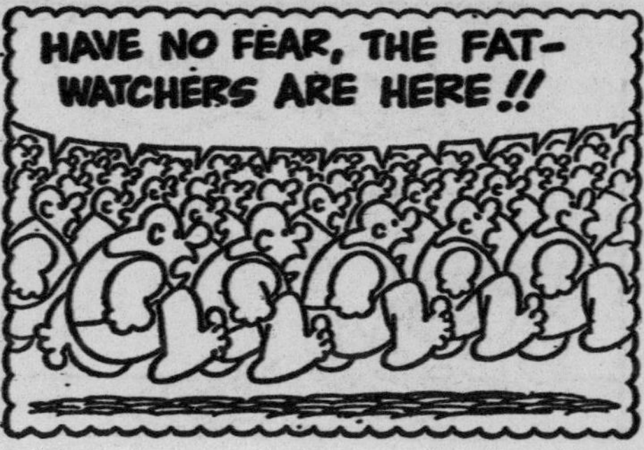
HAVE NO FEAR, THE FAT-WATCHERS ARE HERE!!

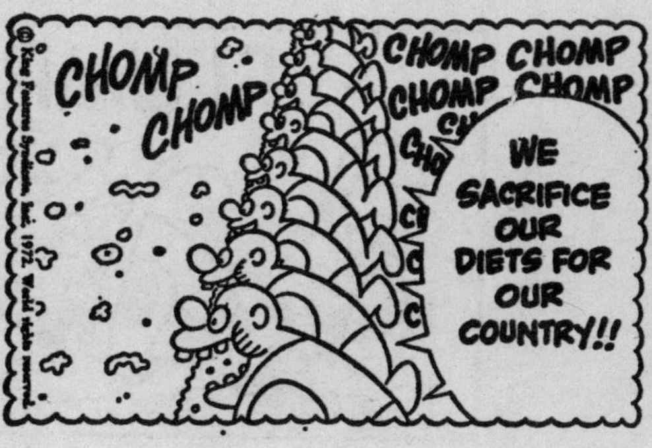
© King Features Syndicate, Inc. 1972. World rights reserved.
CHOMP
CHOMP
CHOMP CHOMP
CHOMP CHOMP
WE SACRIFICE OUR DIETS FOR OUR COUNTRY!!

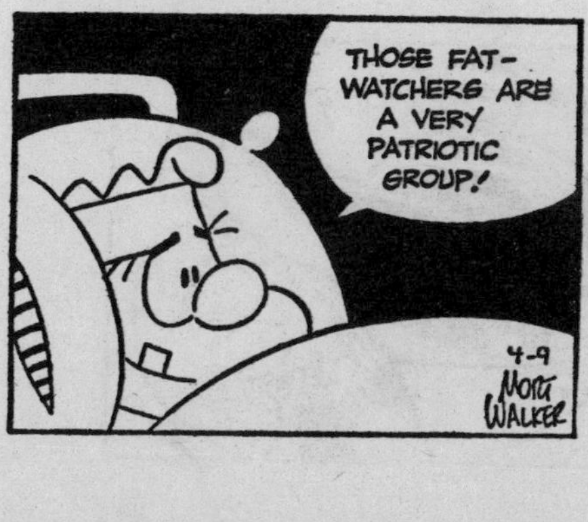
THOSE FAT-WATCHERS ARE A VERY PATRIOTIC GROUP!
4-9
MORT WALKER

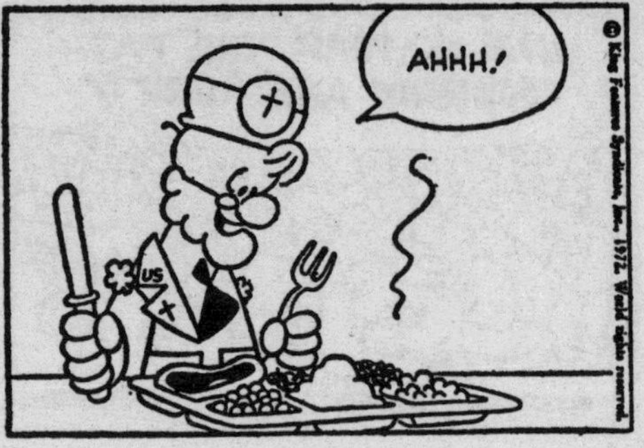
AHHH!
© King Features Syndicate, Inc., 1972. World rights reserved.

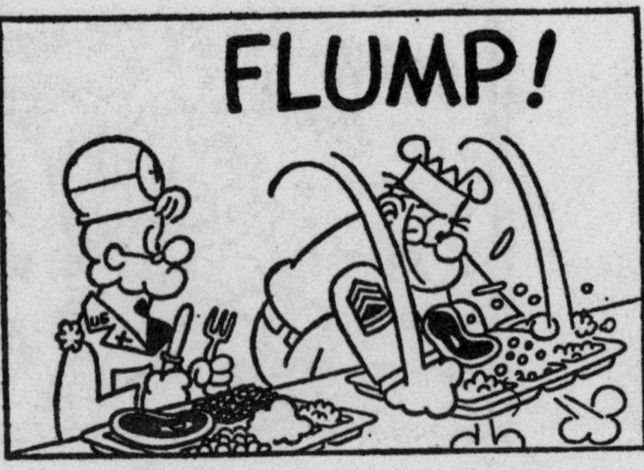
FLUMP!

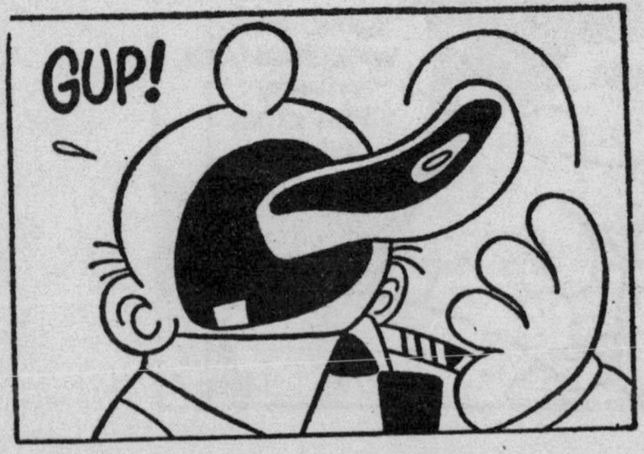
GUP!

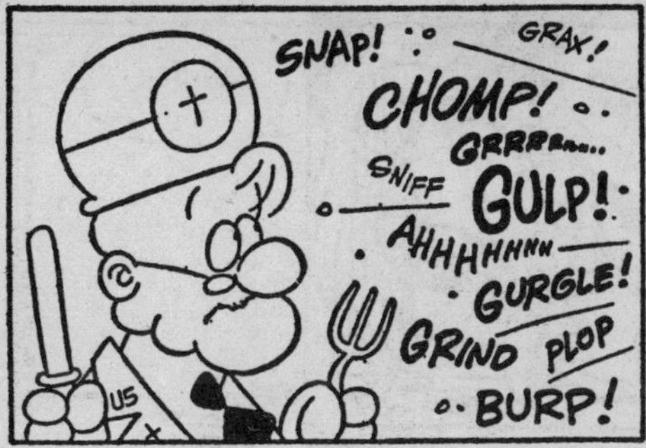
SNAP!
GRAX!
CHOMP!
GRRRR.....
SNIFF
GULP!
AHHHHHHH
GURGLE!
GRIND
PLOP
BURP!

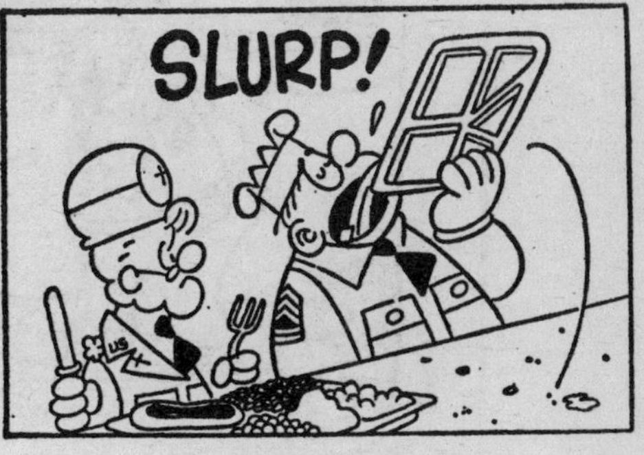
SLURP!

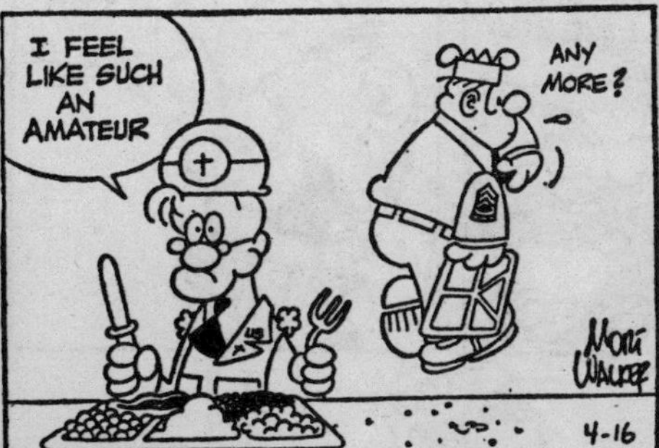
I FEEL LIKE SUCH AN AMATEUR
ANY MORE?
MORT WALKER
4-16

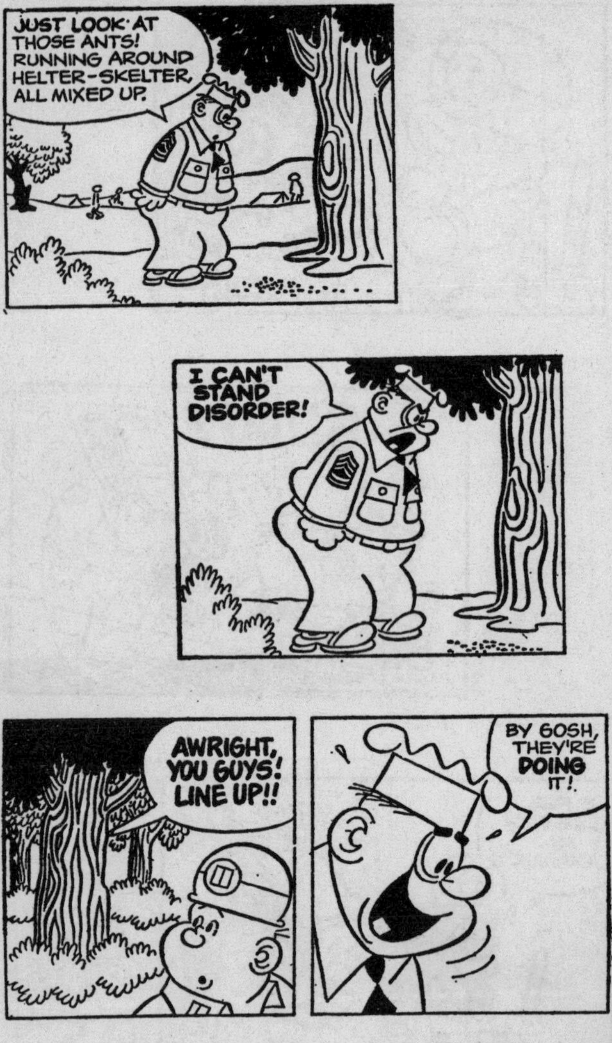
JUST LOOK AT THOSE ANTS! RUNNING AROUND HELTER-SKELTER, ALL MIXED UP.
I CAN'T STAND DISORDER!
AWRIGHT, YOU GUYS! LINE UP!!
BY GOSH, THEY'RE DOING IT!

LET'S GO, ONE, TWO, THREE! EYES FRONT!
© 1959, King Features Syndicate, Inc., World rights reserved.

YOU THERE, WITH THE DROOPY FEELERS! STRAIGHTEN UP!
THAT'S BETTER! NOW WE'LL.. ULP!
GOTCHA!
MORT WALKER

THERE MUST BE A BILLION OF 'EM!! AND I'M THE LEADER!
OF COURSE, SERGEANT
8-9

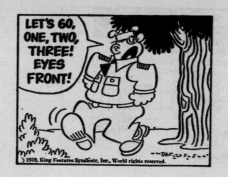

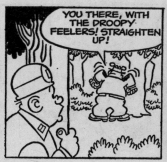

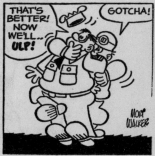

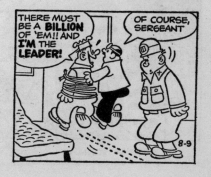

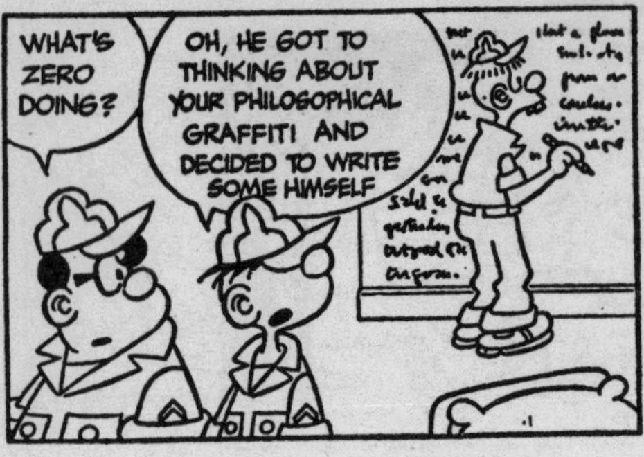
WHAT'S ZERO DOING?
OH, HE GOT TO THINKING ABOUT YOUR PHILOSOPHICAL GRAFFITI AND DECIDED TO WRITE SOME HIMSELF

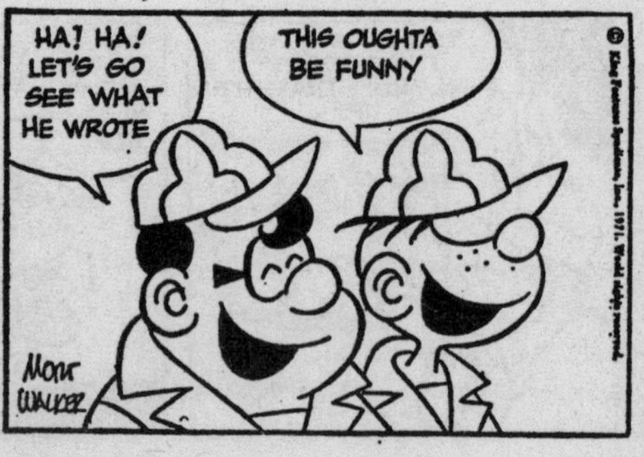
HA! HA! LET'S GO SEE WHAT HE WROTE
THIS OUGHTA BE FUNNY
MORT WALKER
© King Features Syndicate, Inc. 1971. World rights reserved.

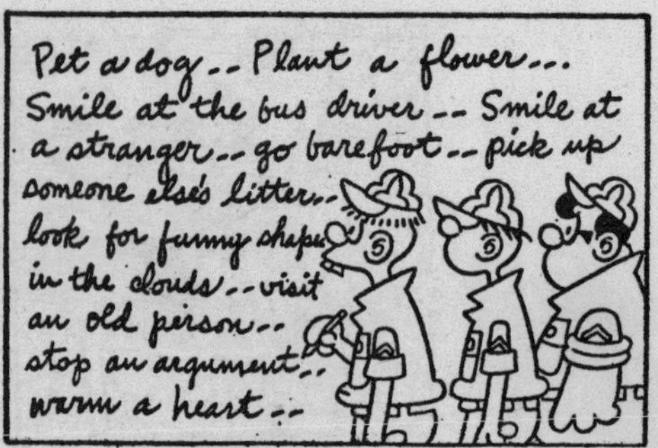
Pet a dog.. Plant a flower... Smile at the bus driver.. Smile at a stranger.. go barefoot.. pick up someone else's litter.. look for funny shapes in the clouds.. visit an old person.. stop an argument.. warm a heart..

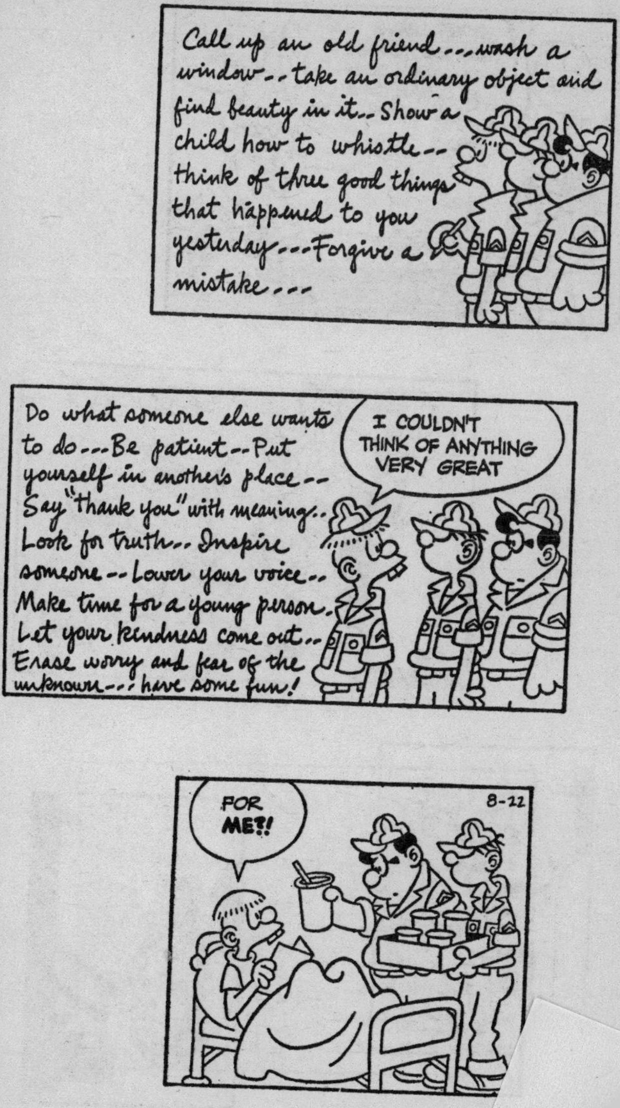
Call up an old friend...wash a window..take an ordinary object and find beauty in it..Show a child how to whistle--think of three good things that happened to you yesterday---Forgive a mistake---
Do what someone else wants to do---Be patient--Put yourself in another's place--Say "thank you" with meaning..Look for truth..Inspire someone--Lower your voice..Make time for a young person..Let your kindness come out..Erase worry and fear of the unknown--; have some fun!
I COULDN'T THINK OF ANYTHING VERY GREAT
FOR ME?!
8-22

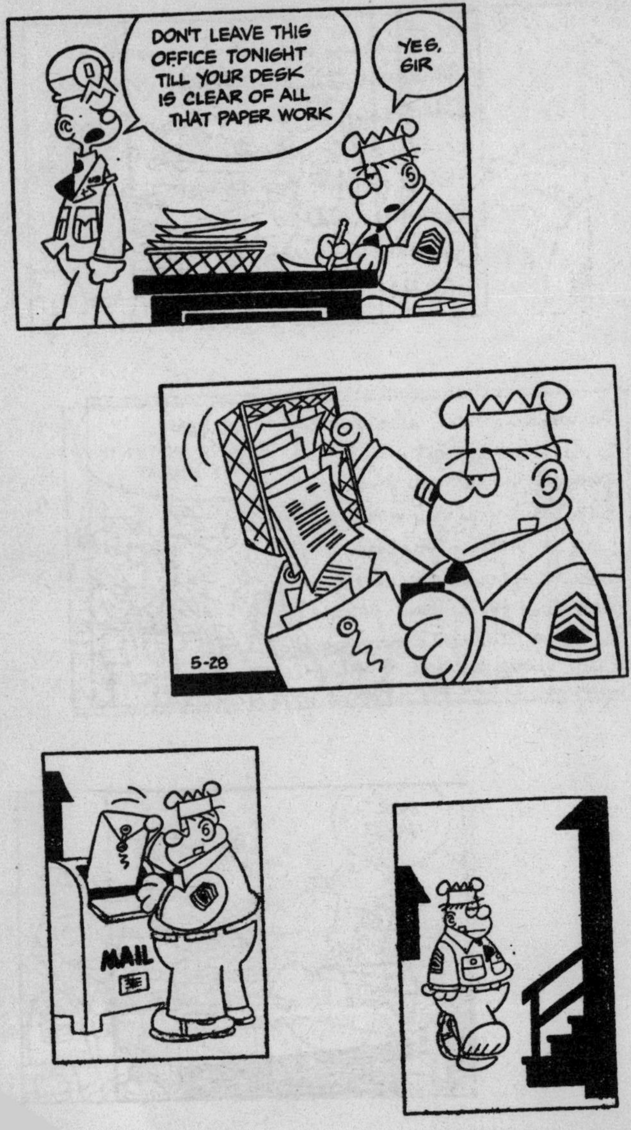
DON'T LEAVE THIS OFFICE TONIGHT TILL YOUR DESK IS CLEAR OF ALL THAT PAPER WORK
YES, SIR
5-28
MAIL

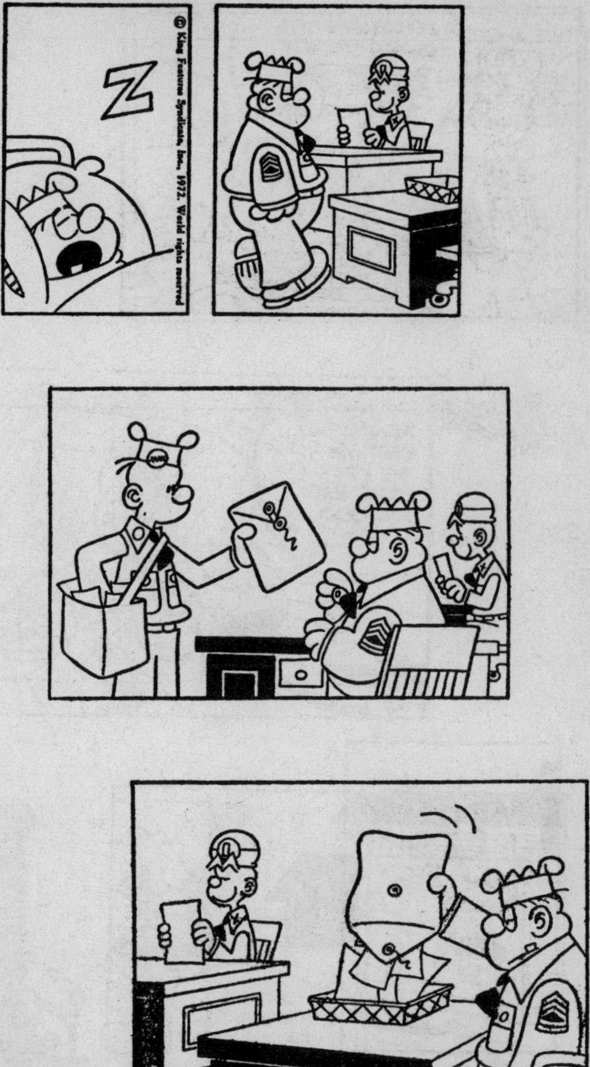
Z
© King Features Syndicate, Inc., 1972. World rights reserved

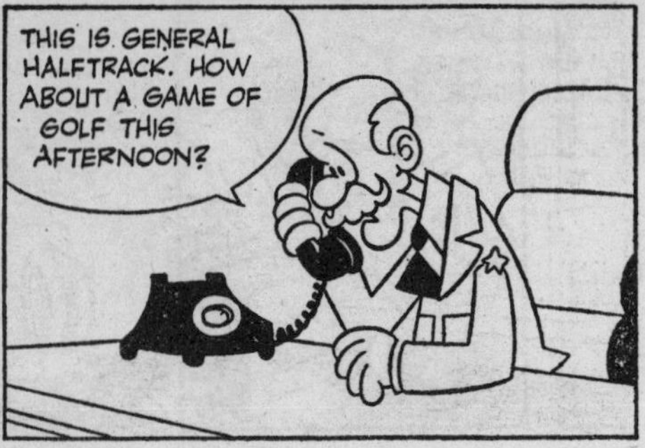
THIS IS GENERAL HALFTRACK. HOW ABOUT A GAME OF GOLF THIS AFTERNOON?

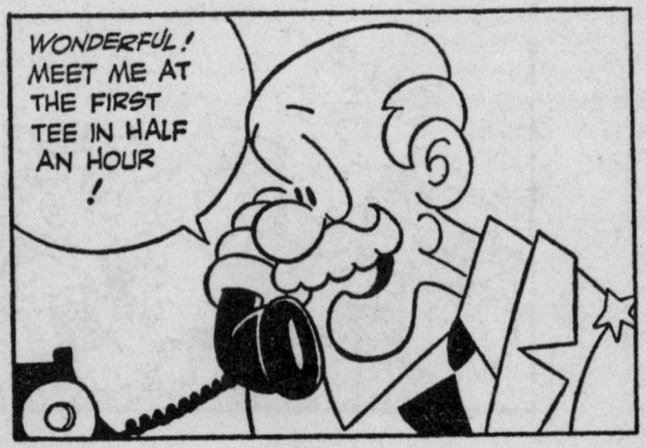
WONDERFUL! MEET ME AT THE FIRST TEE IN HALF AN HOUR!

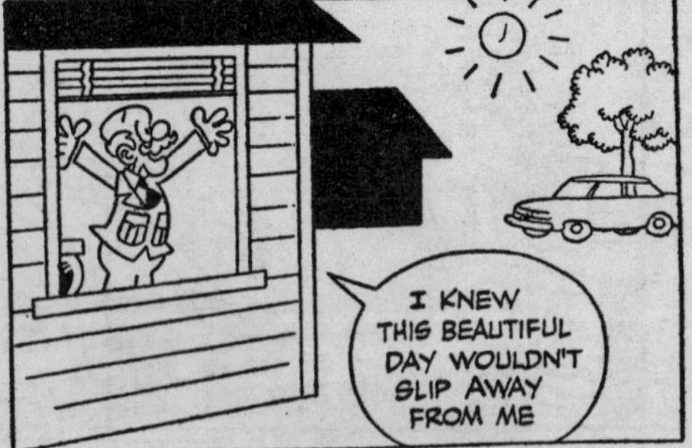
I KNEW THIS BEAUTIFUL DAY WOULDN'T SLIP AWAY FROM ME

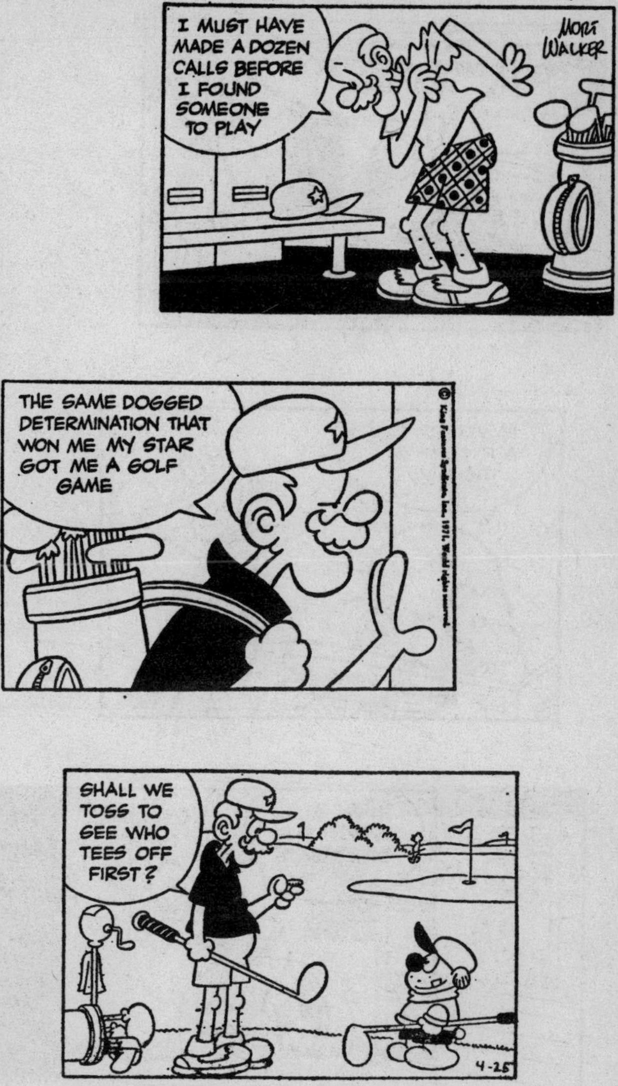
I MUST HAVE MADE A DOZEN CALLS BEFORE I FOUND SOMEONE TO PLAY
MORT WALKER
THE SAME DOGGED DETERMINATION THAT WON ME MY STAR GOT ME A GOLF GAME
© King Features Syndicate, Inc. 1971. World rights reserved.
SHALL WE TOSS TO SEE WHO TEES OFF FIRST?
4-25

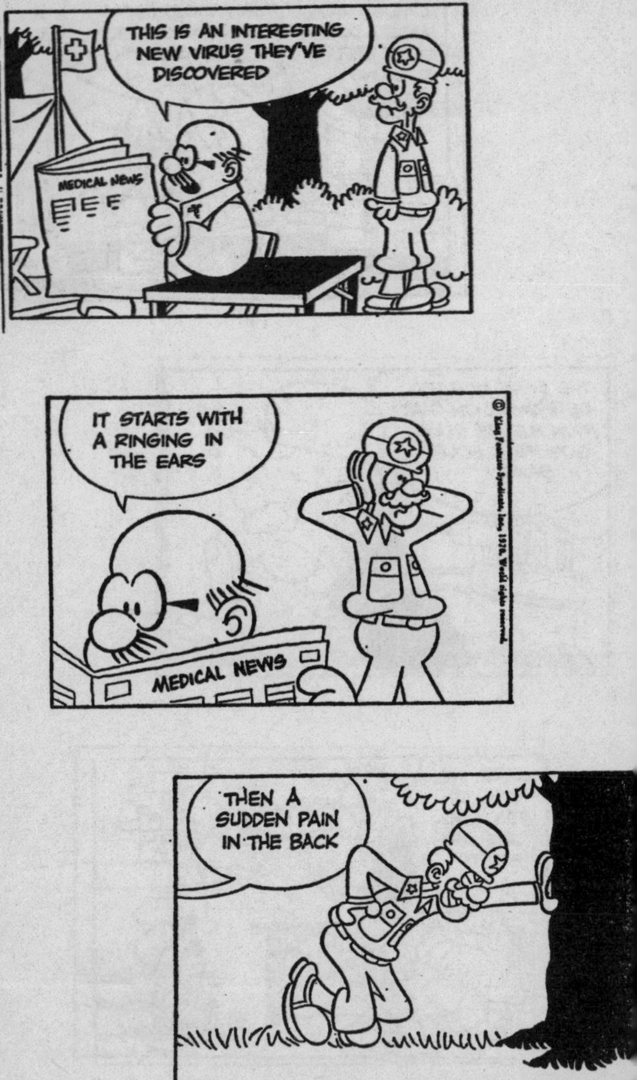
THIS IS AN INTERESTING NEW VIRUS THEY'VE DISCOVERED
MEDICAL NEWS
IT STARTS WITH A RINGING IN THE EARS
MEDICAL NEWS
THEN A SUDDEN PAIN IN THE BACK

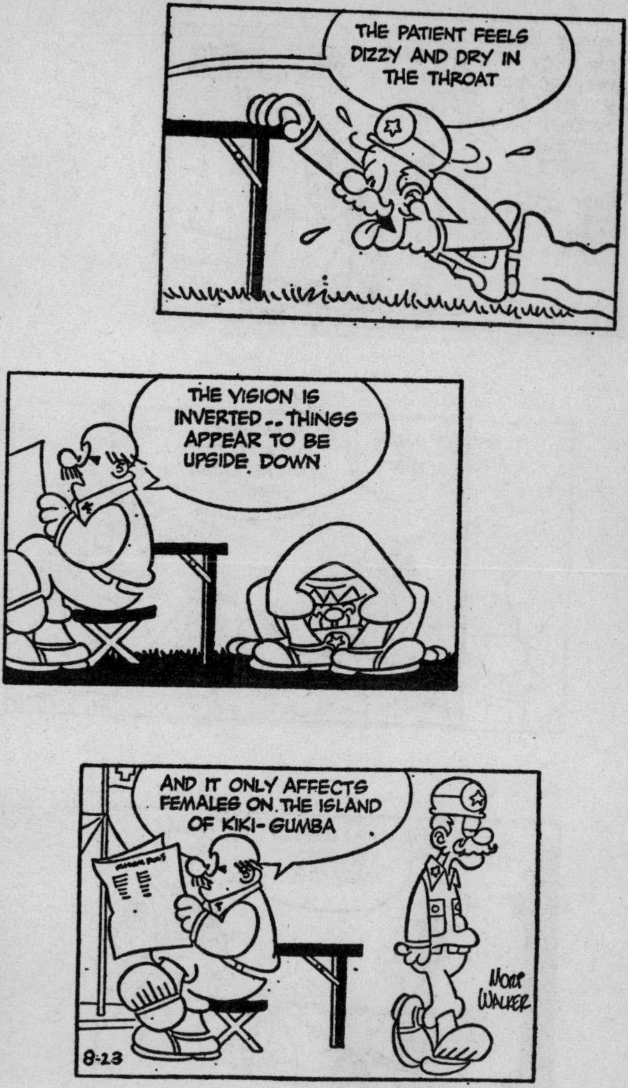
THE PATIENT FEELS DIZZY AND DRY IN THE THROAT
THE VISION IS INVERTED.. THINGS APPEAR TO BE UPSIDE DOWN
AND IT ONLY AFFECTS FEMALES ON THE ISLAND OF KIKI-GUMBA
MORT WALKER
8-23

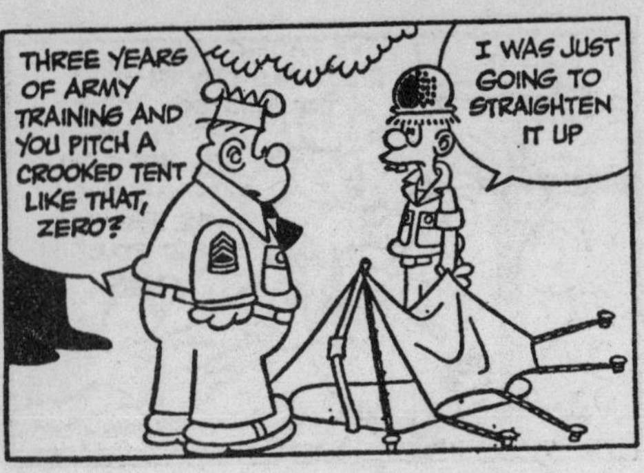
THREE YEARS OF ARMY TRAINING AND YOU PITCH A CROOKED TENT LIKE THAT, ZERO?
I WAS JUST GOING TO STRAIGHTEN IT UP

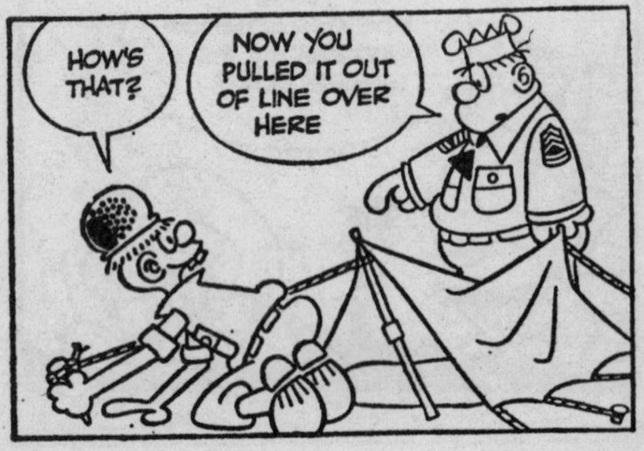
HOW'S THAT?
NOW YOU PULLED IT OUT OF LINE OVER HERE

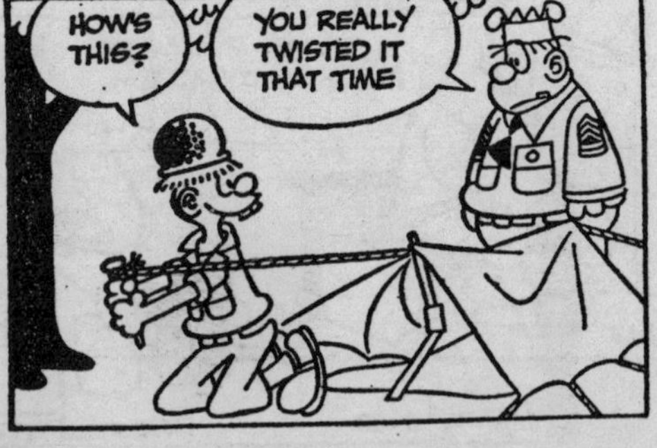
HOW'S THIS?
YOU REALLY TWISTED IT THAT TIME

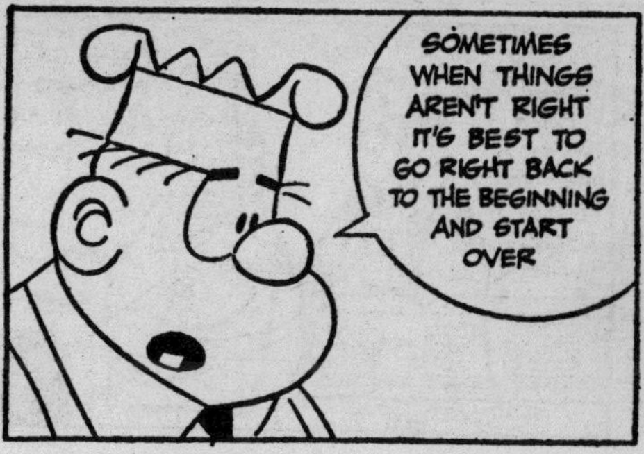
SOMETIMES WHEN THINGS AREN'T RIGHT IT'S BEST TO GO RIGHT BACK TO THE BEGINNING AND START OVER

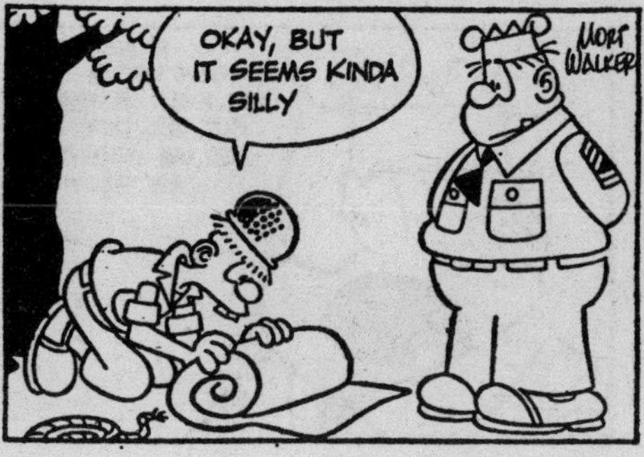
OKAY, BUT IT SEEMS KINDA SILLY
MORT WALKER

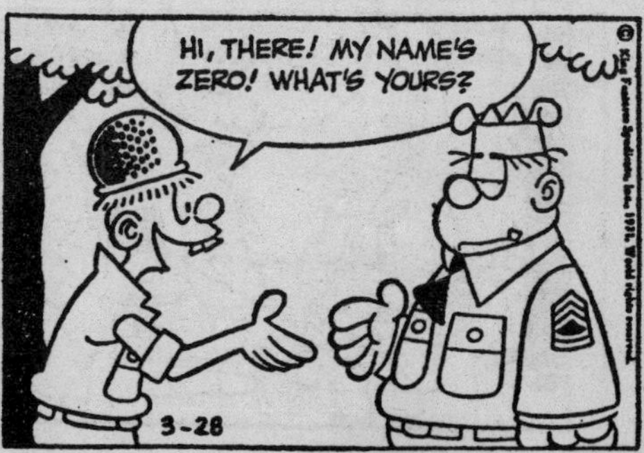
HI, THERE! MY NAME'S ZERO! WHAT'S YOURS?
© King Features Syndicate, Inc. 1981. World rights reserved.
3-28

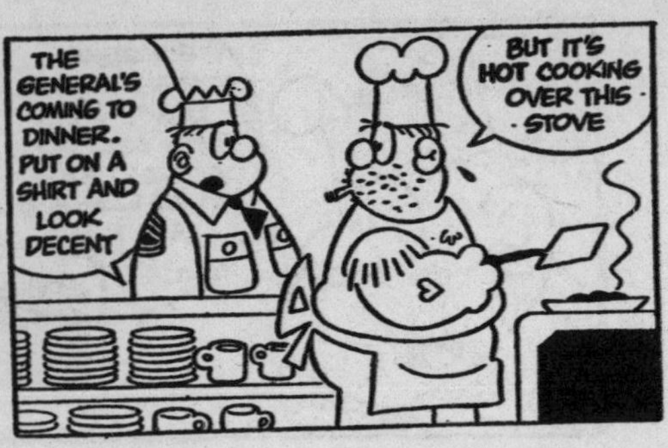
THE GENERAL'S COMING TO DINNER. PUT ON A SHIRT AND LOOK DECENT
BUT IT'S HOT COOKING OVER THIS STOVE

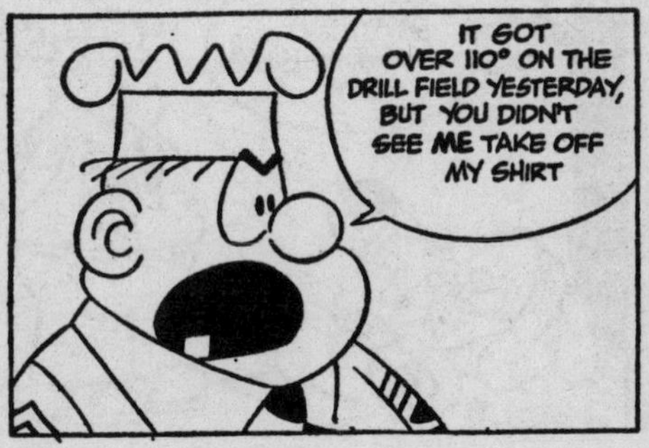
IT GOT OVER 110° ON THE DRILL FIELD YESTERDAY, BUT YOU DIDN'T SEE ME TAKE OFF MY SHIRT

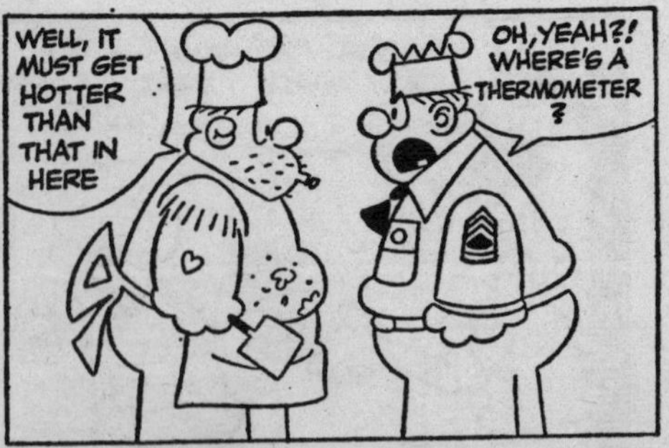
WELL, IT MUST GET HOTTER THAN THAT IN HERE
OH, YEAH?! WHERE'S A THERMOMETER ?

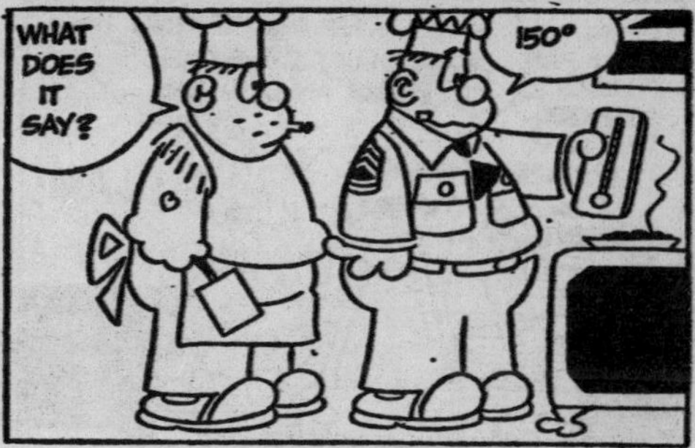
WHAT DOES IT SAY?
150°

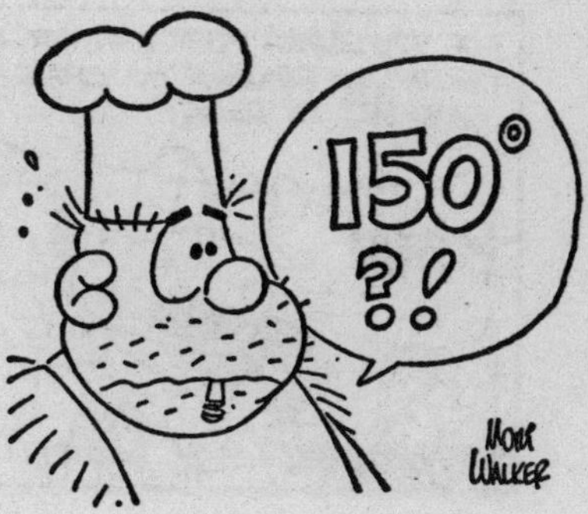
150° ?!
MORT WALKER

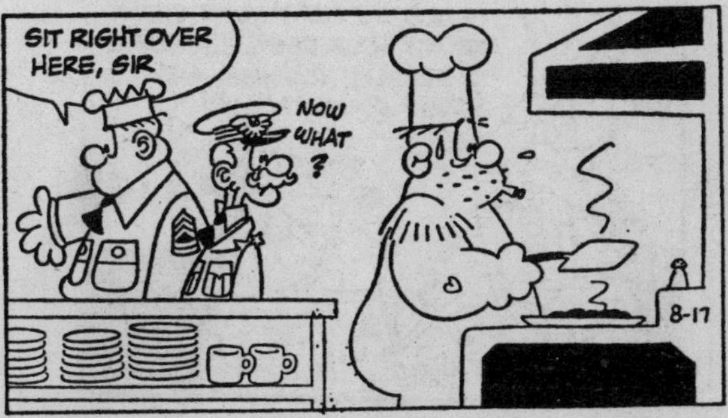
SIT RIGHT OVER HERE, SIR
NOW WHAT ?
8-17

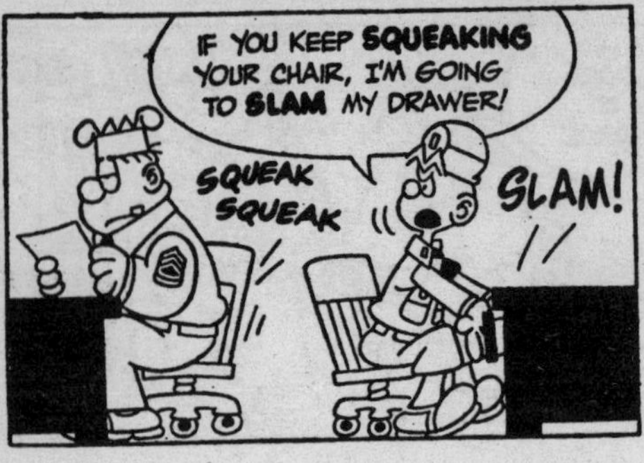
IF YOU KEEP SQUEAKING YOUR CHAIR, I'M GOING TO SLAM MY DRAWER!
SQUEAK SQUEAK
SLAM!

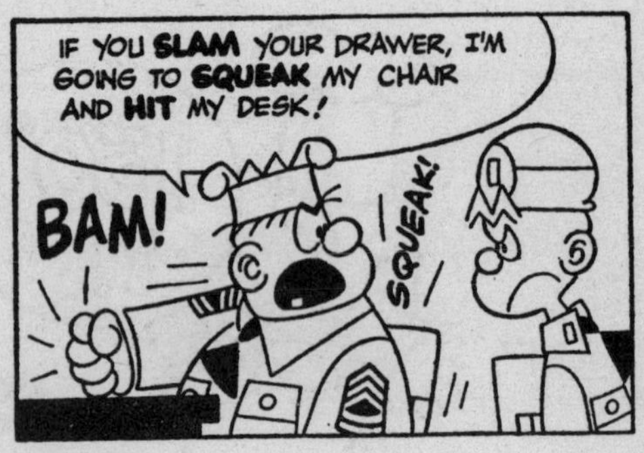
IF YOU SLAM YOUR DRAWER, I'M GOING TO SQUEAK MY CHAIR AND HIT MY DESK!
BAM!
SQUEAK!

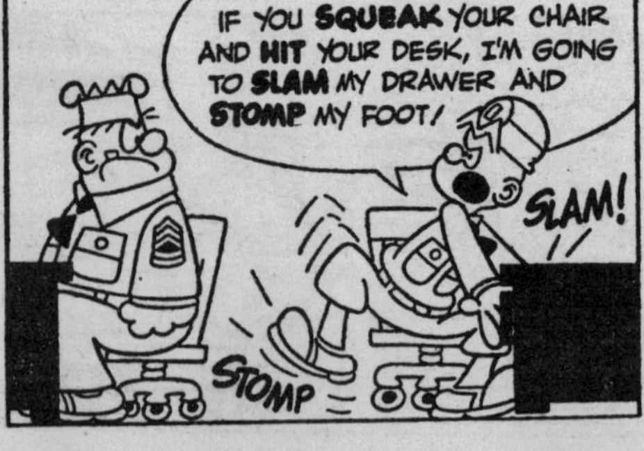
IF YOU SQUEAK YOUR CHAIR AND HIT YOUR DESK, I'M GOING TO SLAM MY DRAWER AND STOMP MY FOOT!
SLAM!
STOMP

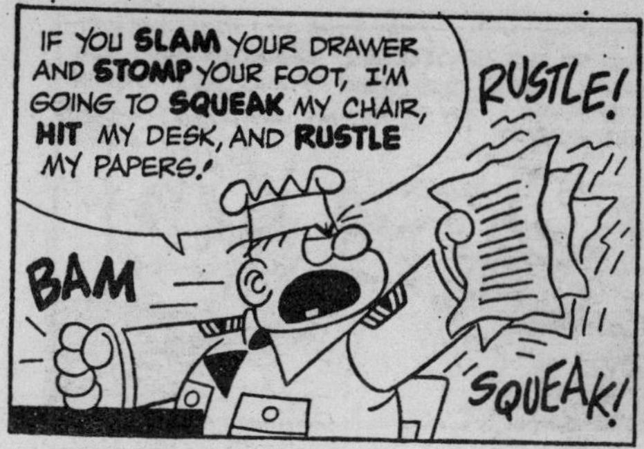
IF YOU SLAM YOUR DRAWER AND STOMP YOUR FOOT, I'M GOING TO SQUEAK MY CHAIR, HIT MY DESK, AND RUSTLE MY PAPERS!
RUSTLE!
BAM
SQUEAK!

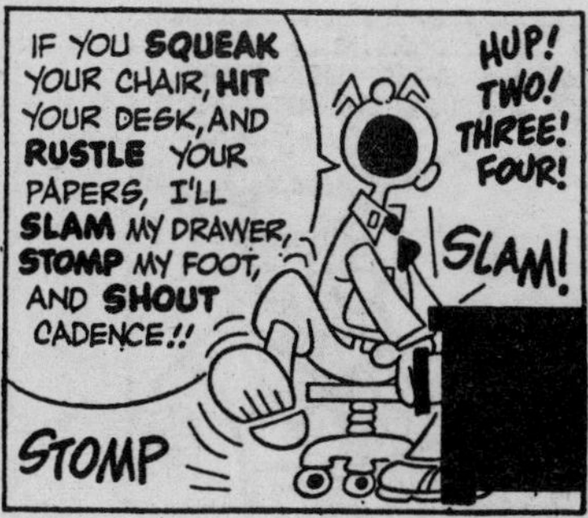
IF YOU SQUEAK YOUR CHAIR, HIT YOUR DESK, AND RUSTLE YOUR PAPERS, I'LL SLAM MY DRAWER, STOMP MY FOOT, AND SHOUT CADENCE!!
HUP! TWO! THREE! FOUR!
SLAM!
STOMP

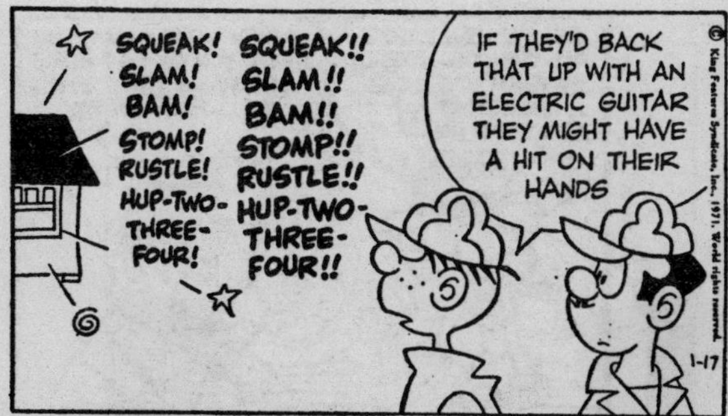
SQUEAK! SLAM! BAM! STOMP! RUSTLE! HUP-TWO-THREE-FOUR!
SQUEAK!! SLAM!! BAM!! STOMP!! RUSTLE!! HUP-TWO-THREE-FOUR!!
IF THEY'D BACK THAT UP WITH AN ELECTRIC GUITAR THEY MIGHT HAVE A HIT ON THEIR HANDS
© King Features Syndicate, Inc., 1971. World rights reserved.
1-17

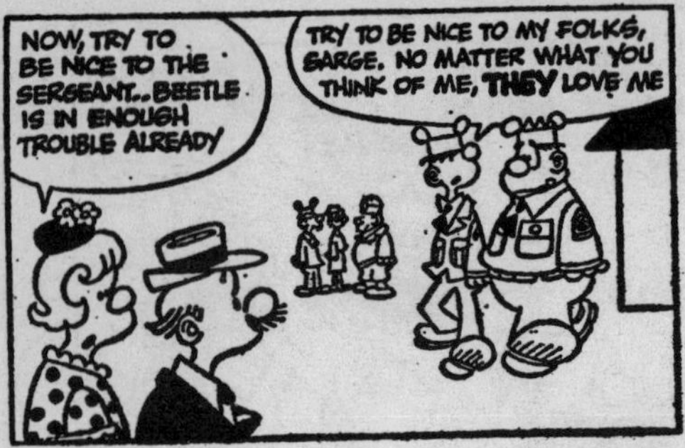
NOW, TRY TO BE NICE TO THE SERGEANT.. BEETLE IS IN ENOUGH TROUBLE ALREADY
TRY TO BE NICE TO MY FOLKS, SARGE. NO MATTER WHAT YOU THINK OF ME, THEY LOVE ME

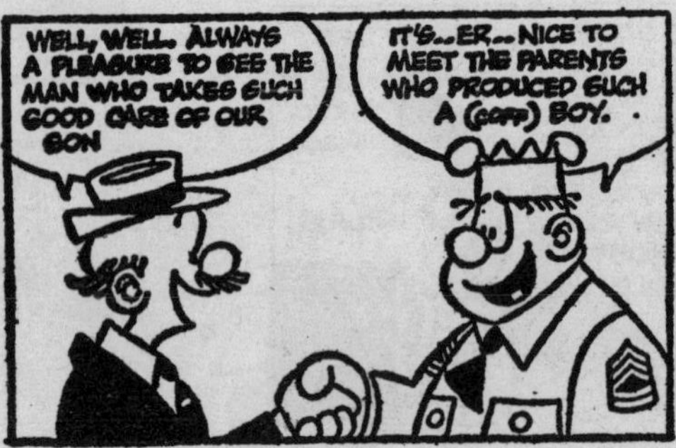
WELL, WELL. ALWAYS A PLEASURE TO SEE THE MAN WHO TAKES SUCH GOOD CARE OF OUR SON
IT'S..ER.. NICE TO MEET THE PARENTS WHO PRODUCED SUCH A (COFF) BOY.

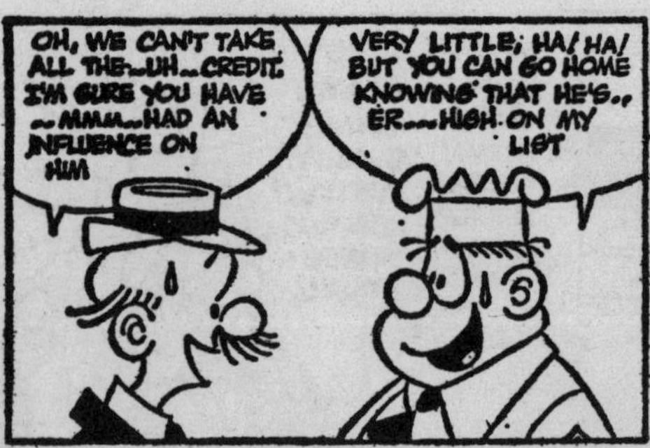
OH, WE CAN'T TAKE ALL THE..UH..CREDIT. I'M SURE YOU HAVE ..MMM..HAD AN INFLUENCE ON HIM
VERY LITTLE; HA! HA! BUT YOU CAN GO HOME KNOWING THAT HE'S.. ER...HIGH ON MY LIST

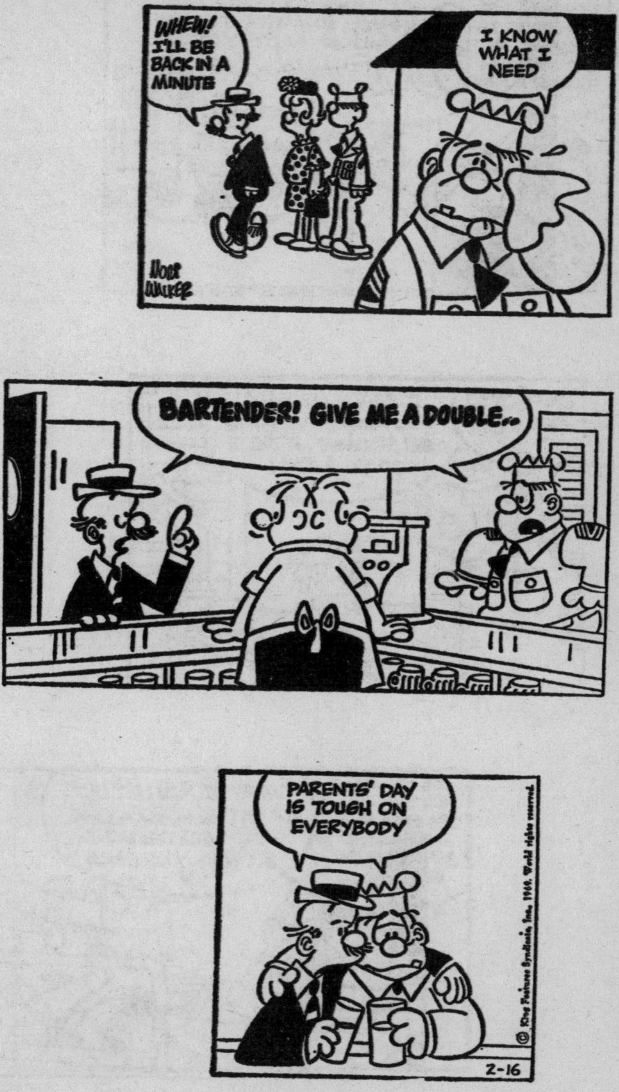
WHEW! I'LL BE BACK IN A MINUTE
I KNOW WHAT I NEED
MORT WALKER
BARTENDER! GIVE ME A DOUBLE..
PARENTS' DAY IS TOUGH ON EVERYBODY
© King Features Syndicate, Inc., 1969. World rights reserved.
2-16

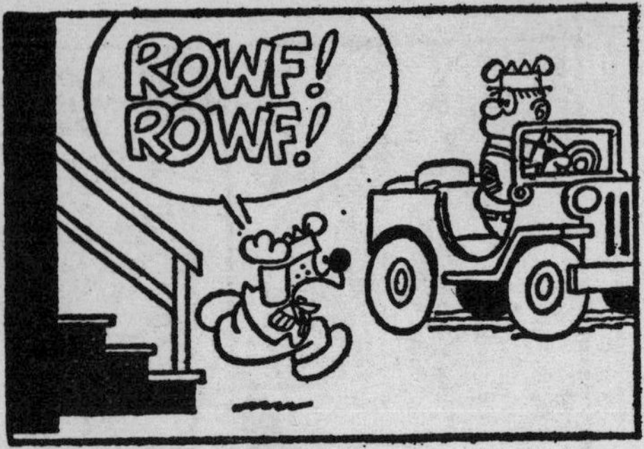
ROWF! ROWF!

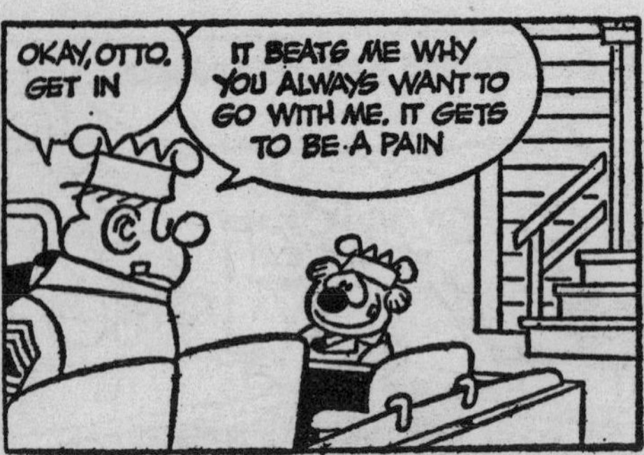
OKAY, OTTO. GET IN
IT BEATS ME WHY YOU ALWAYS WANT TO GO WITH ME. IT GETS TO BE A PAIN

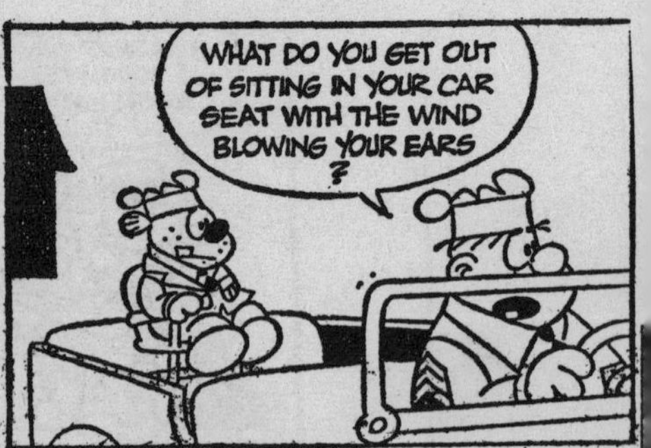
WHAT DO YOU GET OUT OF SITTING IN YOUR CAR SEAT WITH THE WIND BLOWING YOUR EARS ?

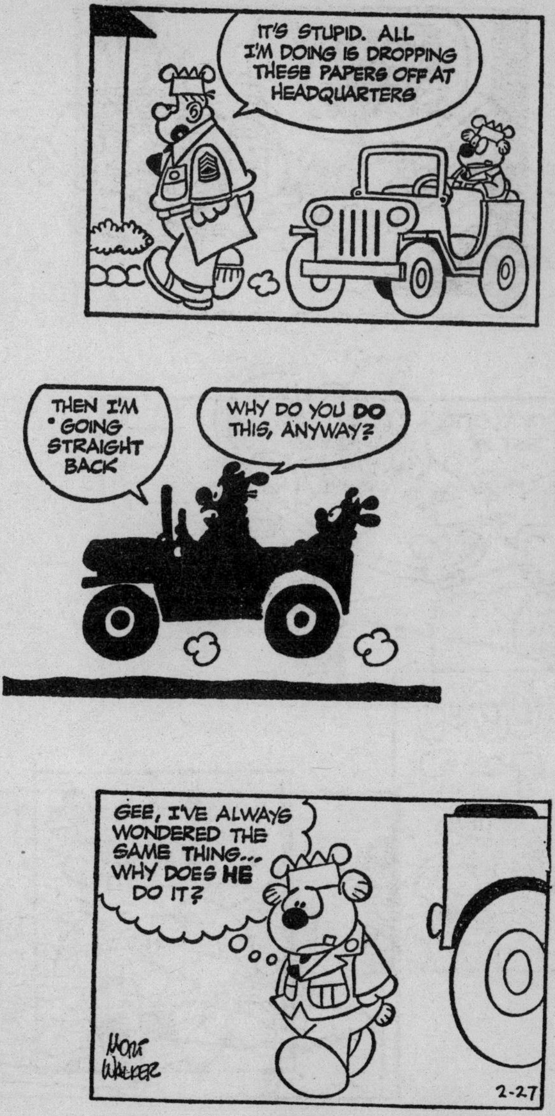
IT'S STUPID. ALL I'M DOING IS DROPPING THESE PAPERS OFF AT HEADQUARTERS
THEN I'M GOING STRAIGHT BACK
WHY DO YOU **DO** THIS, ANYWAY?
GEE, I'VE ALWAYS WONDERED THE SAME THING... WHY DOES **HE** DO IT?
MORT WALKER
2-27

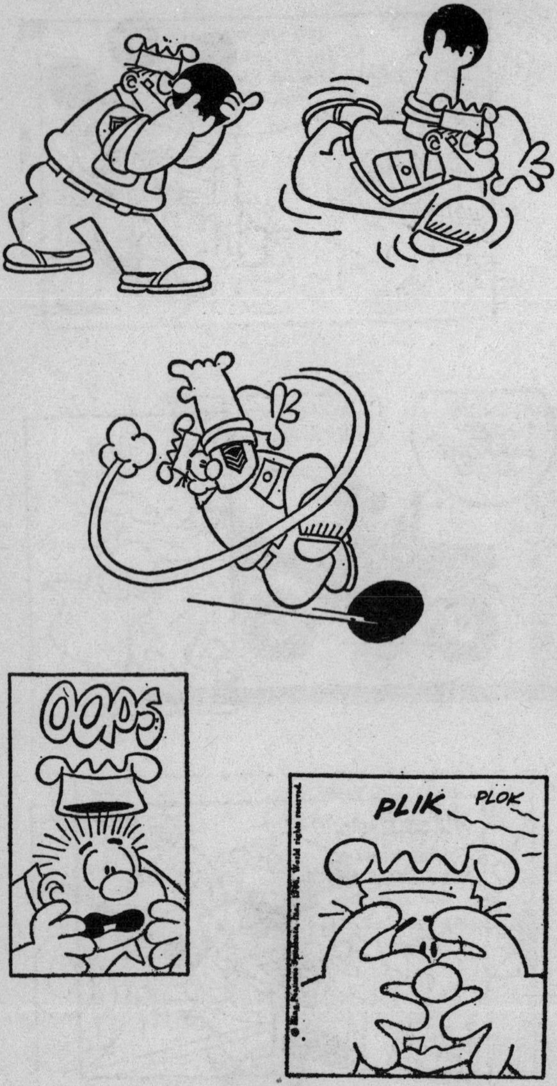
OOPS
PLIK
PLOK
© King Features Syndicate, Inc., 1986. World rights reserved.

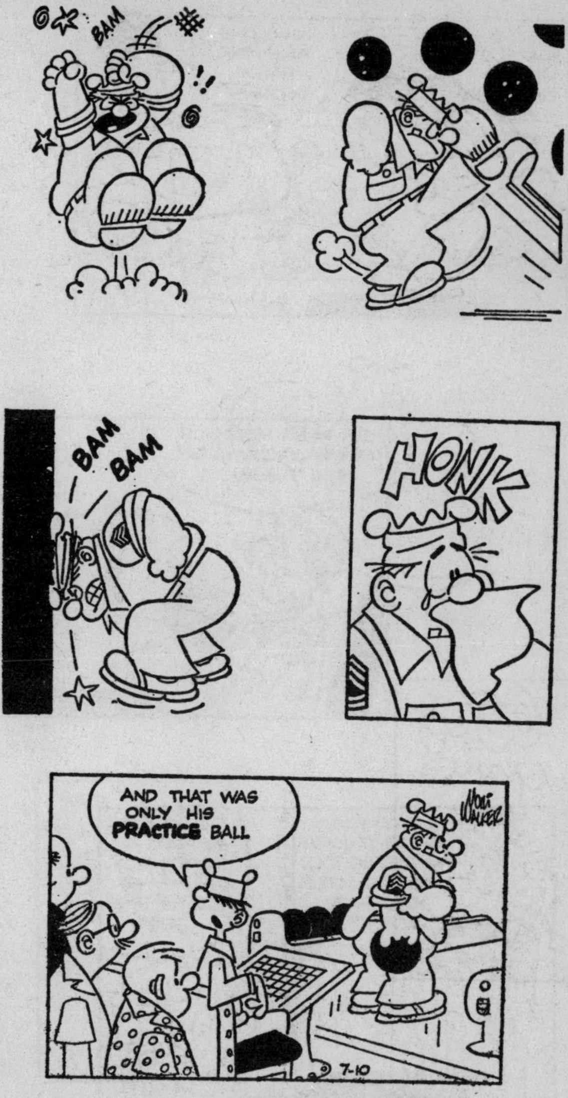
BAM
BAM
BAM
HONK
AND THAT WAS ONLY HIS PRACTICE BALL
MORT WALKER
7-10

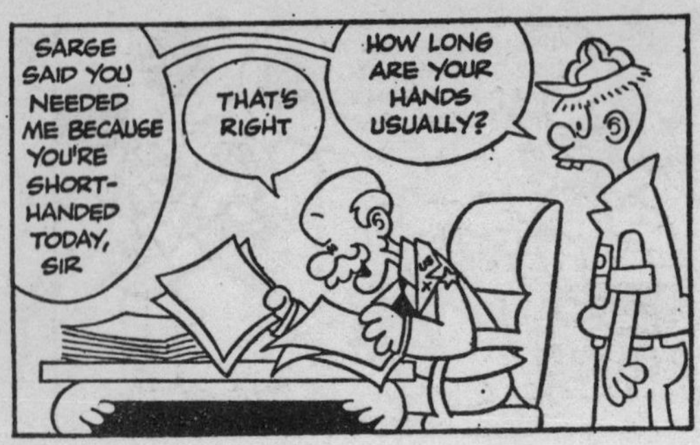
SARGE SAID YOU NEEDED ME BECAUSE YOU'RE SHORT-HANDED TODAY, SIR
THAT'S RIGHT
HOW LONG ARE YOUR HANDS USUALLY?

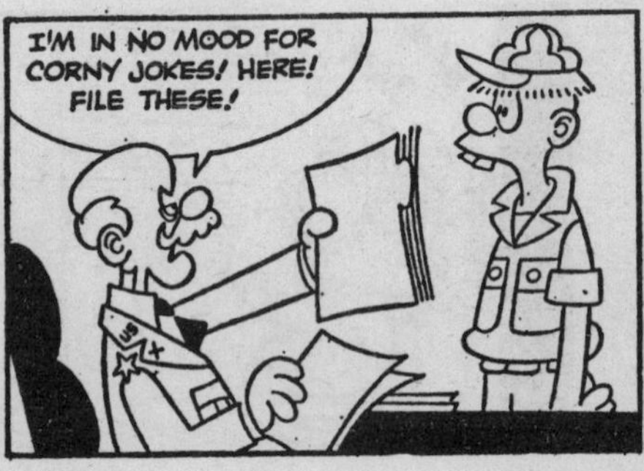
I'M IN NO MOOD FOR CORNY JOKES! HERE! FILE THESE!

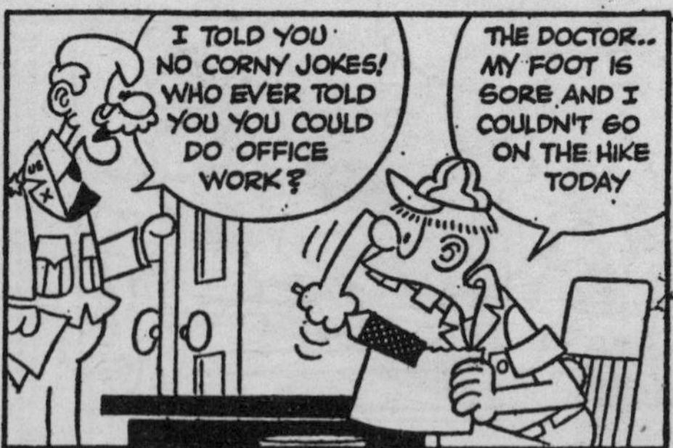
I TOLD YOU NO CORNY JOKES! WHO EVER TOLD YOU YOU COULD DO OFFICE WORK?
THE DOCTOR.. MY FOOT IS SORE AND I COULDN'T GO ON THE HIKE TODAY

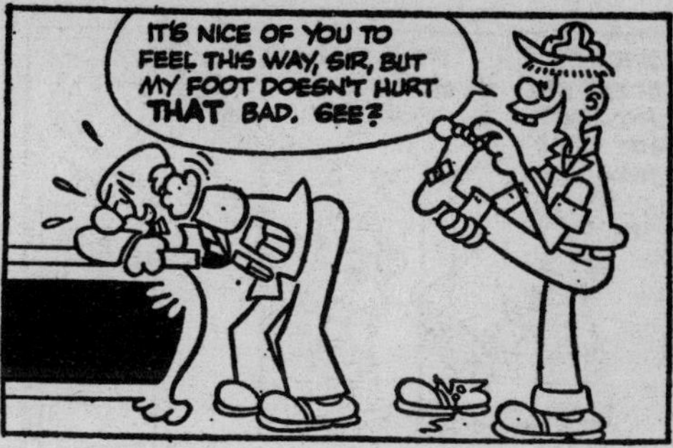
IT'S NICE OF YOU TO FEEL THIS WAY, SIR, BUT MY FOOT DOESN'T HURT THAT BAD. SEE?

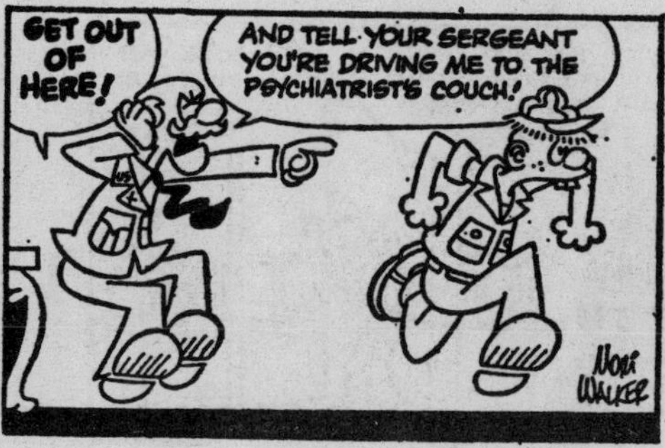
GET OUT OF HERE!
AND TELL YOUR SERGEANT YOU'RE DRIVING ME TO THE PSYCHIATRIST'S COUCH!
MORT WALKER

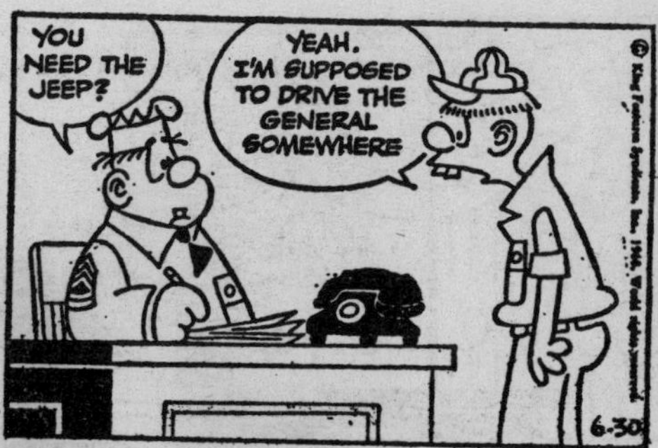
YOU NEED THE JEEP?
YEAH. I'M SUPPOSED TO DRIVE THE GENERAL SOMEWHERE
6-30

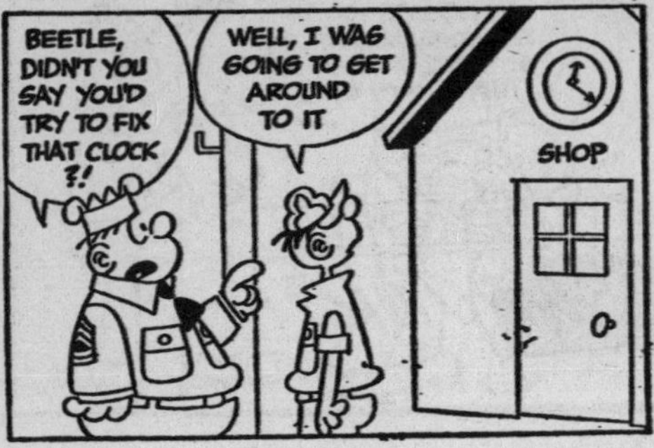
BEETLE, DIDN'T YOU SAY YOU'D TRY TO FIX THAT CLOCK ?!
WELL, I WAS GOING TO GET AROUND TO IT
SHOP

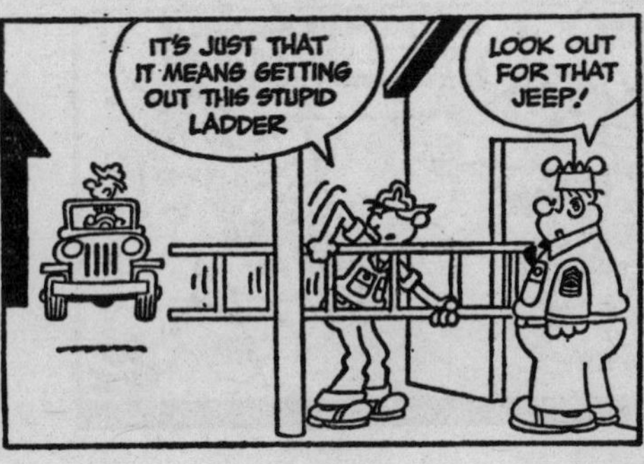
IT'S JUST THAT IT MEANS GETTING OUT THIS STUPID LADDER
LOOK OUT FOR THAT JEEP!

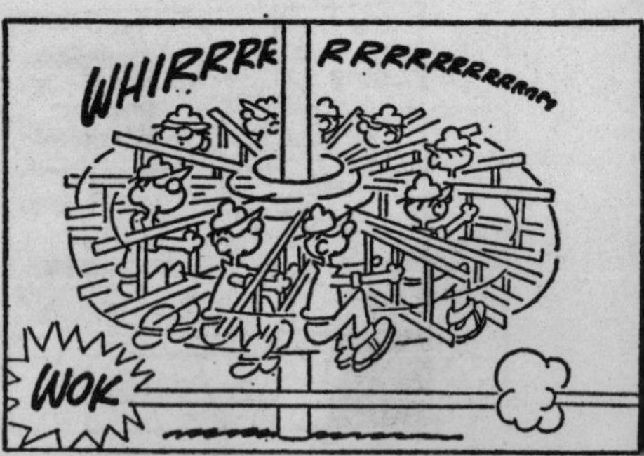
WHIRRRRRRRRRRRRRRMM
WOK

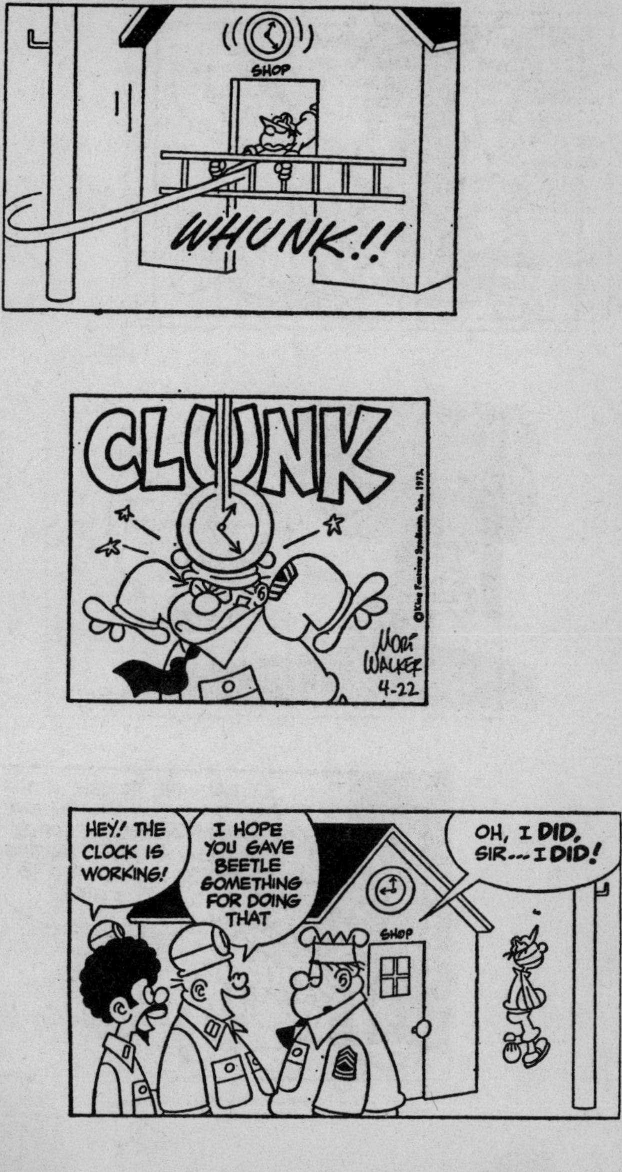
SHOP
WHUNK!!
CLUNK
©King Features Syndicate, Inc. 1973.
MORT WALKER 4-22
HEY! THE CLOCK IS WORKING!
I HOPE YOU GAVE BEETLE SOMETHING FOR DOING THAT
OH, I DID, SIR... I DID!
SHOP

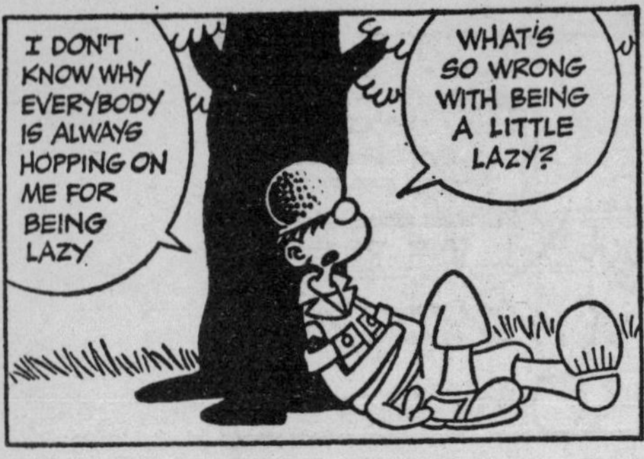
I DON'T KNOW WHY EVERYBODY IS ALWAYS HOPPING ON ME FOR BEING LAZY
WHAT'S SO WRONG WITH BEING A LITTLE LAZY?

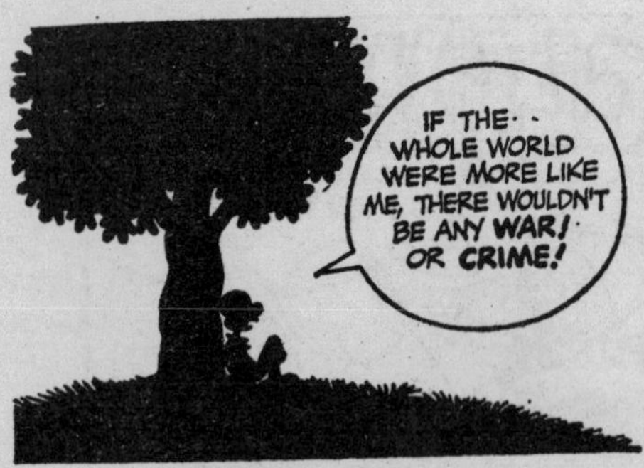
IF THE · · WHOLE WORLD WERE MORE LIKE ME, THERE WOULDN'T BE ANY WAR! OR CRIME!

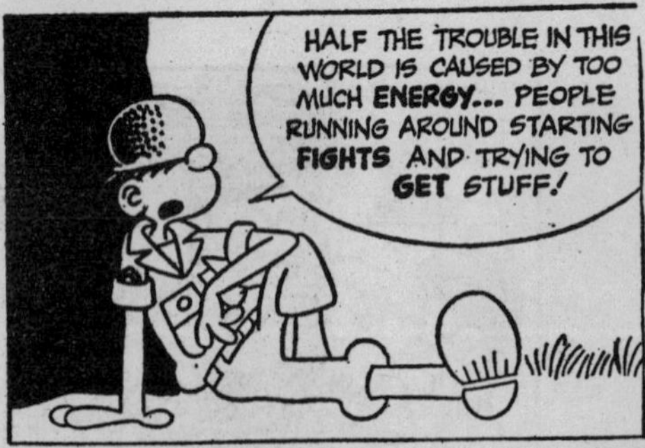
HALF THE TROUBLE IN THIS WORLD IS CAUSED BY TOO MUCH ENERGY... PEOPLE RUNNING AROUND STARTING FIGHTS AND TRYING TO GET STUFF!